MW00849336

"*Love, Jean* offers us an extraor_____
integration dysfunction directl_____
Ayres to her teenage nephew, Pมาหานิ .... : มมมมp shares his recollections of the pain and suffering he endured due to his sensory integration and learning problems, as well as the life changing improvements he experienced as a result of his therapy. Although all of Dr. Ayres' work attests to her brilliance as a neuroscientist, psychologist and occupational therapist, there is no better work to attest to the deeply compassionate and extremely thoughtful approach that embodied her care of children and parents. Throughout the book, Zoe Mailloux's beautiful description of the therapeutic process provides a road map for parents of children, as well as adolescents and adults who experience sensory integration dysfunction, as they embark on a course of assessment and intervention. Everyone will enjoy this rare opportunity to 'visit' with Jean Ayres."

JANE KOOMAR, PHD, OTR/L, FAOTA
EXECUTIVE DIRECTOR
OCCUPATIONAL THERAPY ASSOCIATES — WATERTOWN, P.C.

"*Love, Jean* is the beautiful story of Philip Erwin, a lonely, misunderstood young man with sensory integration dysfunction and his *"Aunt Jeanie,"* Dr. A. Jean Ayres, the scientist who pioneered the diagnosis and treatment of this disorder. Successfully treated long distance through correspondence with Dr. Ayres, Philip also bravely learns survival strategies to cope with his disability. Alluded to, but not detailed, is Dr. Ayres' parallel courageous struggle, facing the onslaught of criticism, ridicule and scholarly exile that accompanied her brilliant new theories and practice. With illuminating commentary by Zoe Mailloux MA, OTR, *Love, Jean* lends powerful insight into Dr. Ayres' compassionate qualities and ground breaking work that led her to develop a theory and science that continues to change the lives of millions of children and adults world-wide. This book will touch the hearts of parents, children and therapists who live or work with individuals who have sensory processing disorders."

LUCY JANE MILLER, PHD, OTR
EXECUTIVE DIRECTOR, THE KID FOUNDATION
ASSOCIATE PROFESSOR OF REHABILITATION MEDICINE AND PEDIATRICS
UNIVERSITY OF COLORADO HEALTH SCIENCES CENTER

"Three voices harmonize in this revelatory song about a boy's evolution from a cowering misfit to a confident man. A. Jean Ayres' letters reveal her thoughts about her research, her own sensory needs, and her family relationships. Philip's reminiscences reveal the pain, hope and exhilaration as he follows Aunt Jeanie's long-distance therapy plan. Zoe Mailloux's commentaries make known what parents can expect from occupational therapy using sensory integration techniques. Altogether uplifting!"

CAROL STOCK KRANOWITZ, MA
AUTHOR OF *THE OUT OF-SYNC CHILD*

Love, Jean

Inspiration for Families Living with Dysfunction of Sensory Integration

❖

A. JEAN AYRES, PHD, OTR

PHILIP R. ERWIN

ZOE MAILLOUX, MA, OTR, FAOTA

CRESTPORT PRESS

CALIFORNIA

LOVE, JEAN
Inspiration for Families Living With Dysfunction of Sensory Integration
By A. Jean Ayres, Philip R. Erwin, Zoe Mailloux

This book is published on recycled paper containing post-consumer waste. Crestport Press is a signatory to the Green Press Initiative.

Interior design by Patty Holden Productions.

Crestport Press
5021 Gregory Court
Santa Rosa, CA 95409

Library of Congress Control Number: 2003116484

International Standard Book Number (ISBN) 0-9725098-1-X

TABLE OF CONTENTS

"The inner-directed child grows more successfully than the outer-directed child."

A. JEAN AYRES

The Story Behind This Book

BY BRIAN W. ERWIN

THE CELEBRATION OF MY PARENT'S 80th and 75th birthdays gave all five of my siblings and me the impetus to gather together for the first time in over 15 years. Among us were a rich stew of talents, including an industrial designer, an architect, a mother and craftsperson, a wooden boat builder, a student, and a book publisher. Having this eclectic collection of passions was not unusual for the Erwin and Ayres families, for among our relatives are a cowboy/inventor, an artisan blacksmith, a curator of spiders, and a farmer who founded a college. With rare exception, our family members have combined intellectual pursuits with skilled labor, one not being considered more important than the other.

A central figure in our family was my mother's sister A. Jean Ayres, or "Jeanie" as we knew her. In that magical and unspoken way of families, we found her to be a totally fascinating person whose passion, drive, and wisdom we took for granted. For us she was just our beloved Aunt Jeanie, not an occupational therapist, neurobiologist, and psychologist whose work greatly impacted the world.

We used to look forward to those times at our grandmother's farm in California's Central Valley when Jeanie's visit would overlap with ours. A hush would fall over our normally rambunctious group as we were called, one by one, into the spare bedroom. In a shaded room looking out upon the grape arbor, there was a small table where Jeanie sat. It was like being invited to peer behind the Wizard of Oz's curtain, for neatly arranged on the table were puzzles, balls and jacks, things that stretched, and a large assortment of oddly shaped wooden and wire objects.

She always sat to our left and in her light, reassuring voice she'd invite us to play with her and her unusual toys. She'd put a new toy or game on the table, briefly describe what she wanted us to do with it, and then observe us. Even while we were intensely completing our tasks, we were aware that she had some purpose for us doing them other than to spend time playing with us. Little did we know that we were among her first test subjects in formulating her concepts of sensory integration.

What I remember most vividly about those moments together is that there were no wrong answers. "Oh, well done!" or "That's terrific!" With such words of approval and support ringing in our ears, how could we do anything but look forward to our own private time with this cherished and utterly unique person.

She was unusual in ways that each of our family members was unusual. Like her, many of my siblings and I somehow never fit into the mainstream. And it didn't seem to matter. Our parents established an atmosphere where creativity was nurtured. It wasn't unusual to us that one of the highlights of visiting Jeanie's apartment in Los Angeles was having her holding aloft a formaldehyde-immersed human brain she kept in a large pickle jar on her kitchen counter. She would take the brain out and pass it around, all the while describing the functions of the different lobes. (For us it was little different from the collection of human digits lost by cowboys during rodeos our Uncle Richard, Jeanie's brother, kept in a jar in a shed by his roping arena.) What we knew were that Jeanie was passionate about figuring out how the human brain functioned and that she led a lifestyle that prevented us from being with her as often as we desired.

It is one of our family's ironies that our family moved from California to the New York City metropolitan area when my younger brother Philip was around five years old, and to the best of his or my memories, he never participated in Jeanie's playtime activities on the farm. For while Philip's four older siblings all fell within the normal range of neurological function, Philip suffered from what our own aunt was in the process of labeling dysfunction of sensory integration.

Jean defined sensory integration as a neurobiological process that refers to the detection, assimilation, organization, and use of sensory information to allow individuals to interact effectively with their environment in daily activities at home, school, and other settings. Basically, there is a part of the brain in well-integrated people that takes all of the sensory input reaching the different lobes of our brains (for example, our senses of touch, smell, how our limbs move, etc.), integrates it, and sends it off for our bodies and brain to manipulate. In those born with sensory integration dysfunction, for some reason this centralized sensory integration function doesn't work well, thus not allowing all of what we sense to reach their final, optimal destinations. In the absence of this information flowing freely, it is more difficult for our bodies to maneuver easily and for learning to occur.

Because of the intensity of Jean's professional life and the great distance separating her in California and Philip in

Connecticut, Jeanie was unable to spend the same amount of time with Philip as she had with my siblings and me. Unfortunately, Philip's condition went undiagnosed. For me he was simply a cool younger brother who got easily frustrated. In his moments of frustration, our mother would call him "Phil the Pill" (under her breath, of course) for few of the parenting techniques Dad and she had employed with their older children proved effective with him.

My parents tried everything they could to help Philip. As Philip captures in the following pages, they sent him to alternative schools and summer camps. They took him to medical doctors who said that there was nothing wrong with him. (Thank goodness this occurred before physicians had such an array of pharmacological options for "treating" what is considered aberrant child behavior. I'm sure they would have recommended that Philip be dosed to the gills. This is in contrast to sensory integrative therapy, which is a natural process.) They took him to psychologists, some of whom recommended that Philip be sent to private school. I remember overhearing my parent's pain and frustration. They not only worried about what they could do to help Philip be happier as child, they wondered how he was going to make his way as an adult.

Reentering our lives at this dire moment was our Aunt Jeanie. According to family lore, after listening to our mother describe the advice she was receiving from psychologists, Jeanie shook her head and said that without sensory integration intervention she doubted Philip's condition would improve. That conversation among sisters set in motion the dramatic changes that are captured by Jeanie and Philip in their letters and stories.

All of these memories came flooding back to Philip and me

at the family reunion while we read Jeanie's letters to Philip that Mom had saved for almost 30 years. Philip and I sat alone in a bungalow that last evening and poured through them. For us it was like stumbling upon the Holy Grail, for there captured in writing were not only our aunt's love for her nephew, but a road map for parents written by the pioneer of the theory of sensory integration. It was a map that resonated especially deeply with me.

Ever since I had moved back to California, my wife Christine, our daughters, and I had spent every Thanksgiving on my aunt Carmen and uncle Richard's ranch with Jeanie, her husband Franklin, and my cousin J.D. It was within days after one of these Thanksgivings that we received a letter from Jeanie beginning, "Choosing to run the risk of being seen as a meddlesome relative rather than as one who did not offer information at the appropriate time—" In observing one of our daughters Jeanie suspected that she had dysfunction of sensory integration. Like my brother Philip, our daughter got easily frustrated and was loathe to undertake physical activities that others her age performed easily. Like my parents, we were relieved finally to have a name to put to the source of our daughter's frustration and dove into therapy wholeheartedly. Once again our aunt's love had deeply impacted our lives.

Reading those decades-old letters in that darkened bungalow, Philip and I marveled at Jean's empathy and her ability to describe the complexities of the human brain in ways that we could comprehend. We realized that in Philip's story we had an unusual opportunity to describe sensory integration in ways that would fill other parents with hope for their children.

Back in the mid-1970s there were few occupational therapists or psychologists trained in sensory integration diagnosis and therapy. And, at age 13, Philip was on the outer edges of the age where sensory integration therapy was considered most effective. While it would have been better for Philip had his condition been diagnosed at a younger age (as it is more often today), we realized his memories as a young adult of what life felt like before, during, and after sensory integrative therapy were unique. He could remember what it felt like to have dysfunction of sensory integration and how he coped with it. He could describe how he felt during the different stages of therapy. And, most importantly, he could relay a message of hope to parents that children with dysfunction of sensory integration can lead extremely productive and happy lives. That night Philip volunteered to write stories from his life that would be juxtaposed in *Love, Jean* with Jeanie's letters to him.

To put into context the meaning of the commitment she made to writing to her nephew every two weeks, it is important to understand her physical frailty, her sense of desperation at the passage of time, and the powerful forces aligned against her work and life.

Jean was not blessed with a physically strong body. She never believed that she would lead a long life, causing her to have a focus on work few of us see in any other individual. While through her research she was making all sorts of insights into how the different lobes of the brain function and the central processing role of the vestibular system, she knew that the pace of her discoveries were always being challenged by her sense that she would not live long enough to complete her work and to see it adopted.

One of the more crushing moments in our time together

came one Thanksgiving when she seemed crestfallen. Christine asked her if something was wrong, to which Jeanie responded, "I was just told by the American Medical Association that my work, quote, 'Has no merit.'"

Even after almost 30 years of research, having over 50 research papers published in scientific journals and books published, and energy-sapping lectures all over the planet, her life's work had been judged meaningless by the medical establishment. All we could do was comfort her. It was the only way we could let her feel our support and deep gratitude not only for our sibling's and child's good health, but for the good health of millions of children whose parents chose not to let such intransigent institutions prevent them from seeking help.

Love, Jean was written for parents who know that something is wrong with their child and who choose to do something about it, the therapists who help them, and the teachers, psychologists, and medical doctors who understand and value these children. Its goal is simple: We want you to feel the great love and respect our aunt had for children and the message of hope from one whose life she saved.

If your child has been diagnosed with dysfunction of sensory integration we hope this book will help you feel buoyed. Therapy for dysfunction in sensory integration works! Your child's nervous system will be rearranged and they will, to a greater or lesser degree, feel more comfortable with their surroundings and with other people. For some, it will make learning easier. If our family's history is any example, in time your child's therapy will be like a long-forgotten booster shot: It was something they did when they were young and they've moved on.

As neither Philip nor I are trained in sensory integration theory, diagnosis, or treatment, we are indebted to Zoe Mailloux, who was one of A. Jean Ayres's first research assistants, and her inspirational staff at the Pediatric Therapy Network in Torrance, California. Ms. Mailloux kindly wrote the sections describing the parent's experience with therapy and reviewed this book to ensure its technical accuracy. We, in turn, are donating a percentage of the book's net profits to research undertaken by this non-profit organization.

HOW TO READ THIS BOOK

You sense that something is not right with your child. However, those to whom you've turned—your pediatrician, your child's teacher, other parents—can provide no guidance or insight. Not only can they not put a name to it, they may tell you that nothing is wrong, or that you've done something wrong as a parent. *Love, Jean* is written for you in anticipation of this exact moment.

Jean Ayres believed that parents knew their children best and she greatly valued their insights. Now, through her voice, and those of Philip Erwin and Zoe Mailloux, your insights into your child are acknowledged. The fact that you are reading this book right now could mean that your child and you are preparing to embark on a life-changing journey.

Depending on how you absorb information best, you can read *Love, Jean* one of two ways. You can read it as it is presented, with Jean's, Philip's, and Zoe's voices intermixed. Layer by subtle layer, you will get a peek behind the curtain of what will happen to your child during therapy from the child's and the therapists' perspectives. With Jean's letters you will observe the wealth of knowledge she presents gradually to Philip to help him understand why he's doing what he's doing in therapy and how it's affecting him physically and emotionally. From Philip's stories, you will glean insights into what it feels like to be a child with undiagnosed dysfunction of sensory integration and how therapy completed connections in his brain that have allowed him to lead a fulfilling life. From Zoe's advice, you will get answers in advance telling you what it's like being a parent whose child is undertaking sensory integrative therapy and what you can do to anticipate this process and maximize its impact.

If, on the other hand, you prefer reading information that is presented sequentially, you can read all of Jeanie's letters, followed by reading all of Philip's stories, and then followed by reading all of Zoe's advice. Please don't let the book's form get in the way of you completing it with a richer and deeper understanding of the help your child is about to receive.

Love, Jean is not intended to be the definitive parent's guide to sensory integration. It is meant to be read in tandem with A. Jean Ayres's own guide for parents entitled *Sensory Integration and the Child* and a growing body of other fine books being written for parents.

We wish that you could have known our aunt Jeanie. She was a remarkable and fascinating human being. We also wish there were words in the English language to describe the deep, deep gratitude we feel towards her and the huge impact she has had on our lives. That she found time amidst her precious journey on this Earth to help two of her nephews is a testament to her deep love for her sister Nancy and brother-in-law Richard (our parents) and to their children.

We wish you well on this journey. May therapy for dysfunction in sensory integration improve your child's sense of himself or herself and make it easier for you to be the parent you want to be.

May *Love, Jean* fill you with hope!

Brian Erwin
Publisher and Nephew

The Journey Begins...

❖

PHILIP ERWIN'S JOURNEY towards integrating his brain began on Highway 99, a four-lane highway linking southern and northern California. His mother Nancy had flown to Los Angeles to meet up with her sister Jean Ayres. From there the two sisters drove up to visit their mother, Louise Ayres, who still resided in Visalia, the central San Joaquin Valley town in which they were born and raised on a farm.

While gazing out the car window at the acres and acres of crops growing on the fields lining the highway, Nancy told her sister about a diagnosis a psychologist had recently given Philip: that his behavioral and learning problems were the result of delayed maturation and he would grow out of it. After her sister finished describing the problems Philip was experiencing, Jean sort of shook her head and said that without intervention she doubted that he would outgrow it.

Not too much was said at the time. Nancy believes that Jean wanted to think about the ramifications—the big investment of her time and energy—of the offer she would make soon thereafter to treat Philip from a distance.

And so began Philip's journey.

July 28, 1975

Dear Nancy,

In response to your request for information on having Philip
tested for sensory integration dysfunction, I suggest that you write
an O.T.R. [a registered Occupational Therapist] who was sent to
me last year for three weeks of in-service training, and has quite
a bit of experience at the Churchill School in New York City in
evaluating children with learning disabilities.

The owner of the school, Harry Valentine II, is director of the
Valentine-Kline Foundation, one of the major sources of support
for my current research.

Should you write her, please tell her that I referred you and that
you are my sister. Also please let me know if you plan to do this so
that I can write her and tell her my thoughts on Philip.

If your observation on post-rotary nystagmus is accurate (and
I know how hard it is to be accurate) they are quite significant. No
wonder Philip is having a rough time! The fact that he disliked the
rotation is also significant and suggests that the vestibular input is
not only not reaching its proper destination but is overwhelming
him instead of orienting him and making him feel integrated. The
most miserable children I see are those with that combination but
to a more severe degree. For some time I have felt that his problem
fit into the syndrome of postural and bilateral integration, as
described in my book. I am not sure though. There often is a
heredity component in that problem. I am not sure of the rele-
vance, but in one study on factors that contribute to brain damage

at birth in monkeys, six monkeys whose birth was induced by drugs all had brain damage. There may have been other factors, such as reduced oxygen, that contributed.

The last thing you need to worry about is Philip using knowledge of sensory integrative problems as a crutch. On the contrary, it would probably help him to feel better about himself. I know that it has been helpful to me to be able to determine that I had some brain damage at birth.

I wish you could stop by more often.

You might tell Philip that Franklin says that just about all he ever got on his grammar school report card was "Could do better if he would try." The very words send him into a frenzy, even now.

Love,
Jean

A. JEAN AYRES
TORRANCE, CA

August 25, 1975

Dear Nancy, Dick & Philip,

The therapist I referred Philip to had occasion to call me about several matters and told me briefly about the result of her evaluation of Philip.

Without wanting to be interfering but at the same time wanting to help, I think you should know that it is most likely that Philip has the kind of neurological organization that usually responds to treatment. I say usually because we haven't treated many teenagers—but here is an example: A few years ago I saw a 13-year-old girl who was having trouble in math but not in reading. Like Philip, she seemed to have inherited some very fine genes for language function. I referred her to a therapist for treatment. She saw the therapist once a week and worked one hour a day at home for about six months. I cannot say that she enjoyed what she did, but her math and typing improved. She also felt better about herself.

If I knew somebody in Connecticut whom I felt could do a good job of treating Philip I would refer you to that person. Since I don't, I am offering to treat Philip by mail, providing he would like to do so.

This is what the procedure would involve: I would explain by mail the basic principles and the kind of equipment needed to engage in a series of sensorimotor activities. Most of the equipment I have put together myself, and there isn't anything that I have made that couldn't be made easier and better by at least four members of the Erwin family.

Philip would use this equipment in your backyard or basement not less than half an hour or more than one hour, five times a week for not less than six months and not more than for a year. The activities would involve movement that activates the vestibular system and which require an adaptive (movement) response on Philip's part. When he got dizzy or felt nauseated he would stop that activity and try something else.

Sometime during the 2nd to 4th month of treatment most individuals go through an upsetting period during which they feel less well organized and rebel at the treatment, but once past that stage treatment can be enjoyable. Academic improvement does not appear, usually, until around the fifth month.

Academic improvement cannot be guaranteed, of course, but it is almost certain that physical coordination and feeling of well-being would improve.

The hardest part of being treated under these circumstances is the lack of structure which keeps a person at the task and reminds him that the whole thing is worthwhile. If Philip chooses to follow this suggestion, I would like him to write me every two weeks and tell me how he felt about that activity.

Love to all,
Jean

The Race

BY PHILIP R. ERWIN

MY PARENTS KNEW that something was wrong. Until the fifth grade most things had gone well for me in school. From what I read now in my report cards from that time there were hints that I was going to have trouble. Although I was regarded as a creative child who made friends easily, my teachers consistently remarked that they had difficulty making me put down my book or stop drawing in order to follow the rest of the class through the curriculum. Still, nobody was saying that I *couldn't* do the work. They merely observed that I *wouldn't*. They suggested that perhaps if I tried harder, or if Mom and Dad put some pressure on me, I might do better. I only remember doing the things that I enjoyed and was good at, and feeling annoyed at the injustice of their interruptions.

Sixth grade was a time of great change for me. My family moved from suburban New York to a small town in southern Connecticut. Although we had been moved frequently due to Dad's work, it was the first time that a move had interrupted my scholastic life, forcing me to reestablish my credibility as a cool kid in a new environment. I believe that fifth grade was the last time that I was on the same playing field as other kids. As Jeanie described it to me in one of her letters much later, it wasn't that

I was beginning to fall behind; it was that I was beginning to stand still as others around me moved forward. Only now I would be standing still among strangers. My parents knew that something was happening and made the first of many decisions aimed at finding a place for me where I could learn.

The New School (one of many "New Schools" in the late sixties and early seventies I suppose) was my first stop. There I was allowed to learn in my "own way." My way happened to be reading and drawing and molding in clay—as always. Only now nobody was going to stand in my path. When the staff tried to compel me to learn math they gave me a pile of little colored blocks and said, "Now learn math." I built bridges, houses, cars, and planes. I didn't see the mathematics in the objects I built (for there was none), but it gave me time to bluff. My parents pulled me from The New School because I was miserable there. It was also a wise move, as The New School became the Old School—or better, the *Out of Business School*, when it failed sometime soon thereafter.

The next thing I knew I found myself walking into a large classroom in Weston Public Elementary School well after spring term had begun. The class that I joined was made up of two big groups in a large "open classroom" format. There were lots of kids seated at numerous tables working on neat projects. *Maybe I would be all right.* The morning went just fine. I got to draw and read. I even met a couple of kids who seemed nice. After lunch and recess—a very lonely hour—we reconvened at our desks. The teacher announced that we would be having a race—*sounds like fun, I thought to myself.* The way that the race worked was this: The teacher would write the same multiplication problem on two opposite ends of the blackboard. We were divided into two teams. Two students would run up to the front of the room when they were called. The first one to finish solving the problem would run back to their team and tag the next kid in line. And so on.

No, I didn't go first. That would have been enough to wreck me for life. Instead I went fourth, or seventh—I don't exactly remember. I do remember sitting with my face on fire desperately running over my options. I could feign illness. I could run out the door when my name was called. I could refuse to go up to the front of the room, and when I was sent to the principal's office I could keep going and run away from home.

I felt the tag. I ran up to the board—please, please let it be obvious, two plus two, *anything*. I had no idea how to do the math. I didn't know the times tables. Well, I knew a few that rhymed or made sense like, fives and tens to a limited degree, but not the strange monster on the board facing me. I couldn't recall my own name under these circumstances, much less the few times tables I remembered for their non-mathematical properties. Chalk was scratching on the other end of the board and kids were cheering. I stood and looked like I was trying to think the problem through. Nothing. Redder and hotter. Sweating. Shaking. Humiliated. The other kid tagged out. Cheers. I stood. I turned slightly to the teacher and said, "I don't know how."

There was no escape though. The teacher came over on the premise of "helping" me get started. I wasn't sent back to my seat, I wasn't given a reprieve or a method of escape. Time passed.

"We'll do it together," she said finally. And she solved the math problem while I stood mutely next to her trying to pantomime, "Ah, that's all it was? Heh, O.K., got it."

The walk back to my seat was a long one indeed. I would rather have been naked, although to a certain degree I was. I was stripped of any veneer of pride I might have retained that first day. I was exposed as the fool that I was before I could install my careful public image as "Mr. Artist." Now, I would forever be the new, stupid, incapable kid.

Thereafter, any and all forms of competition became, in my mind, opportunities to fail in front of and in comparison to all of the other kids. My new goals were focused on getting home each day and pretending that there was not going to be a tomorrow.

Of course my mom and dad didn't just abandon me to be sacrificed on the math altar. They had acted upon the suggestions of my teachers over the years and had tried to help me with math, organization, and deadlines. Flash cards worked quite well if we were only worried about me parroting back various combinations of numbers immediately after I had seen them. I could have spoken German the same way. Retention, or worse still, understanding, was what was missing. (To this day tables three, four, six, seven, eight, and anything above one hundred are a new and novel concepts to me each time I give them a shot; I cannot learn my times tables.) Troubles were on the horizon. I had lost a crucial race that day and I would not regain the lost ground for some time.

A. JEAN AYRES
TORRANCE, CA

September 5, 1975

Dear Philip,

I am glad you have decided to engage in a therapy program. A year from now you will be glad of it. When I read your letter I shed a few tears.

While I think of it, I have been referring some high school students with learning problems to a colleague in Arkansas that has a special program for people with isolated learning problems like yours. They rely on a person's strengths rather than his weaknesses for academics. Wish there were a high school like that for you.

My main task now is to try to explain how this therapy works to help learning. I don't blame you a bit for not understanding how sliding down a slide head-first helps math. You don't understand because you and practically everybody else don't know what has to go on in the brain before one can read or do math. And I don't know entirely; I have just enough knowledge to present a little theory that has led to treatment that has helped at least 80% of the boys and girls who have the kind of problem you have. I'll try to help you understand what I do know so that the activities will be more meaningful.

It looks as though your problem—and this is true of most of the learning problems that continue into teen age—particularly involves the vestibular system. The vestibular system has receptors or sensory end organs in a part of the ear. These receptors respond to gravity and movement of the head in space. From an evolutionary standpoint, this is a very old system, and it is one of the first systems to develop in the infant. This sensory system sends messages to many, many parts of the brain—more parts than most of us realize. It even sends messages to that part of the brain that has to do with our emotions. At this point I am guessing that this system has to work reasonably well in some way that is related to helping one side of the brain, or cerebral hemisphere, to communicate with the other side. When this communicating mechanism that is dependent upon the proper function of the vestibular system does not develop correctly, the two sides of the brain do not communicate and each side develops similar skills.

The therapist I referred you to says that your left and right hands are almost equal in fine motor skill. Both cerebral hemispheres have developed skill in directing fine motor work, whereas, if they had been able to communicate better, just the left hemisphere, directing the right hand would have developed the skill and the right hemisphere would have used those neurons for something else. I can't explain exactly what it is in math that requires both hemispheres communicating. It has something to do with the language side having to communicate with the space-visualization side of the brain.

Math, especially the first few years of math, are quite closely related to space perception, and space perception does not develop well unless the vestibular system develops well. This does not seem to be the most important thing with you, though, because you have always shown a most remarkable sense of space, at least from an artistic standpoint.

Now, how do we get that vestibular system working better? We do that by activating the receptors, especially through movement, and most importantly, ask the body to react to that movement. Treatment consists almost entirely of just that.

Some people don't get dizzy soon enough when moved as in rotation. Some people get dizzy too soon. You seem to be of the latter type. That means that your brain is not modulating the sensory input. It is not organizing it. It is upsetting you instead of making you feel well related to the physical world. I have never yet seen a boy (usually it's boys but sometimes it's girls) who was not able to make that situation better. You make it better by making what we call adaptive responses. Most adaptive responses to vestibular stimulation are simply balancing reactions. It is by balancing that the brain learns to organize the vestibular input and to send it to where it is suppose to be going.

So most of the activities I will be recommending are going to be balancing activities, but there will also be a lot of movement to produce the sensory stimulation your brain needs to learn to organize. With many of the boys who don't get dizzy enough, we give them a lot of activities that involve spinning, but I don't recommend them for you because you can't organize those stimuli. But if you ever feel like spinning or rotating, for goodness sake, do it. If it's comfortable, it will help.

There are a couple of important things for you to remember as you treat yourself, Phil. The boys who improve are the ones who really get involved in the activities and work at it. We don't have a motivation problem with the 6 to 10 year olds, for there exists in every brain the drive to relate to the earth through the vestibular system. That relationship is normally accomplished by age 8, and after that the drive seems to diminish and the sensorimotor experiences are less satisfying. Also, when the reorganization occurs in the younger child, it is not as upsetting as in the older child.

But since you are older you will be better able to tell what makes you feel good and what is stressing you too much. When you start doing something that feels good to you, keep at it as long as you can, within reason. Repetition is important in reorganizing the brain. Also, if what you are doing feels good, it is probably making things work better. On the other hand, if what you are doing makes you feel uncomfortable, back off and do the same thing more slowly, more carefully, or more simply. Try to push yourself a little when you feel uncomfortable, for you are working in an area that needs development, but don't push yourself so hard that you make yourself sick or feel dizzy for more than two minutes.

Another thing to remember: When you get fed up and, as you say "Forget it" and stomp to your room, remember—when you can pull yourself together to remember—that you are probably going through a period of reorganization. While it may be upsetting for a while, you at least have the satisfaction of knowing you are working in the area of your brain where there is trouble and you will probably work out some of the trouble.

Phil, sometime send me a piece of your math work, with errors, and also tell me just how you see the problem with math. Is it memory? Not knowing where to put the numbers? Not getting the concept? If you work with concrete objects can you get the idea better? Also, I would like for you to keep me informed about your reactions to the activities.

I'm glad you have a basement; this work is pretty hard on the floor. The first thing you will need is a scooter board. Use a board about 14 x 16 inches. It doesn't have to be that wide, but I like them fairly wide so the front wheels can be set in quite a way so that you won't be so apt to run over your fingers. Ride this scooter board on your tummy a lot. It is especially important that you do things that give you accelerated motion that stimulates the movement receptors and give you the sensory input you need. If you have room to make a ramp about 18 inches high that you can ride down, that is a good way to get accelerated motion. But if your basement is small, don't bother; get the accelerated motion by pushing against the wall with your feet. (That's the way I ride my scooter board, which I do several times a week and feel the good effects for several hours.) You may want to put garden gloves on to protect your hands against the cement. If your basement is narrow you can push yourself back and forth from wall to wall. If you weary of the task, pile up some cartons to knock down as you ride the scooter. Or hang a ball from the ceiling and hit it as you go by. If you tire quickly, it is because the vestibular input is not getting to the muscles that arch the back and extend the legs. I don't think your problem will be that, though. Please let me know how long you can ride the scooter board before you become fatigued. This will help me to know how you are reacting.

Another way to make movement more comfortable is to increase sensory input from joints and muscles, especially those along the spinal column. To do this, have someone give you resistance to rolling. As you roll on the floor, have someone hold back your head as you try hard to move against resistance, also hold back your shoulders, or your hips, or your legs. The resultant effort on your part creates sensory impulses from the muscles that tend to inhibit the vestibular nuclei so that you don't get so dizzy.

Please write me about every two weeks, Phil, and tell me what you have been doing and how it makes you feel so that I can get an idea as to what is going on in your brain. And my final comment for a while is, at this point, these activities are more important than math.

Love,
Jean

Something is Not Right

BY ZOE MAILLOUX

HELLO, MY NAME IS Mrs. _____ and I am calling about my child _____.

JEREMY. *He is eight months old and something is not right. His pediatrician says that he is growing and developing fine, but we are having a terrible time at home. He never sleeps more than two hours at a time, as every little noise wakes him up. He likes to nurse, but he won't take a bottle and he spits out most of the foods we give him. Jeremy needs to be held all of the time, but only by me, and he screams when someone else comes near him. I feel so bad, because he just seems unhappy all the time. The rest of the family thinks that I am spoiling Jeremy by holding him and going to him during the night. I have tried letting him cry, but he will cry all night long if I leave him alone and I have the feeling that he really needs to be held. I feel like I am going crazy. I never thought it would be so hard to have a baby.*

SARA, *who is five years old. She will be starting kindergarten this fall and we are worried about how she will do. Sara's teachers at preschool said that she seemed very bright, but that she really struggled with what they called "motor" skills. She avoided color-*

ing and drawing even though most of the other girls seemed to really like those activities. We have always noticed that Sara is clumsy. She is constantly spilling things and bumping into people. She seemed to notice how poorly she was doing compared to the other girls at her little gymnastics and dance classes, so we stopped going. Sara still needs help dressing herself and refuses to even try fastening buttons or snaps. She had some friends in preschool, but she started being "bossy" with them so she doesn't seem to have many friends now. We think that Sara will like the academic challenges in kindergarten, but we are worried about what will happen when she is expected to write letters and numbers and we think there is a good chance she will just sit on the bench during recess, rather than let the other children see how poorly she does in sports and games.

MICHAEL. *Michael is seven years old and he is in the second grade. We cannot figure out what is going on with him. Everyone agrees that Michael is a smart boy, but there are certain things at school that he cannot seem to grasp. Reading is especially hard for him. Michael also has so much trouble organizing his belongings. He is forever losing things and just seems like he is "lost in space." It is a good thing that he has such a great personality! He is funny and quick witted, so he can usually cover up his weaknesses. He is not bad at sports, but for some reason it is taking him forever to learn to ride a bicycle and he still cannot seem to master swimming. Homework is really a nightmare! It takes Michael forever to finish his work, especially if he needs to copy anything. When Michael was tested at school, the psychologist said that he did not score low enough in any area to qualify for special help. But something is definitely wrong. He tries so hard and still can't seem to do well in school. I am so afraid that he is going to give up and stop trying altogether.*

I receive messages like these everyday at my clinic. Countless therapy clinics across the globe hear similar stories on a regular basis. As it turned out, all of these parents were describing sensory integrative problems in their children, but they did not know what to call it. Sometimes problems like those described above are not related to a sensory integrative disorder. However, it is more common that a sensory integration problem does exist and that it is mislabeled, misunderstood, or missed entirely.

A. JEAN AYRES

TORRANCE, CA

September 28, 1975

Dear Philip,

Good heavens, Phil, I can't do math either! I had no idea 8th grade math was so advanced. It looks more like high school math to me. At any rate, you know enough about math to cope with any mathematical demands made on an ordinary life once you get through high school. I don't even know what an additive inverse is. But it was good for me to have to struggle with the problems to try to figure out (for my sake as well as yours) just what it is about the demands of math that are related to communication between the two hemispheres of the brain, which is where I think the problem lies. It is clear that anything that complicated needs both hemispheres working together. The way I am conceptualizing it now, the right hemisphere is having to conceive of the problem as a whole while the left hemisphere is having to deal with the details. The two don't work together very well because the vestibular system isn't making its contribution. That is all just a hypothesis that I am formulating to try to understand learning disabilities and the effect the vestibular system has on them. I am sure it is more complicated than anything I can conceptualize at this point.

I am glad you are off to a good start on your therapy. Here are my thoughts on the timing of your work. I doubt if you will feel any positive effects for at least 5 months. As soon as you get a headache, get dizzy or nauseated, stop what you are doing and do something that does not require rotation. I am glad you can take the linear motion. As you ride the belly board you might try turning around 2 or 3 times at the end of each run. That way you wouldn't build up the sensations that make you uncomfortable but would get the stimulation you need.

Even though you don't notice effects of a positive nature for some time, the influence on the brain is there immediately, probably facilitating transmission of impulses between neurons. For that reason, the ideal time to do the work would be before school and before homework. It doesn't matter how you break it up time wise, otherwise. I wouldn't think you would want to do it right before or after a meal, though, because of its effect on your stomach. If it doesn't bother you, it's O.K.

I don't know much about teaching math, but it seems to me that if I were a tutor I would try to use blocks of wood to illustrate the principles involved in some of those formulas. I think you might get them spatially more easily than numerically.

Love,
Jean

Homework

BY PHILIP R. ERWIN

GOING TO SCHOOL seemed to be a very grownup activity. It was a practice that conveyed status. At least that was my view as I, the preschooler, watched my older siblings come and go so independently. They came home from long days away speaking strange languages and carrying tall stacks of thick and important-looking books. While I complied with "bedtime"—often by dusk with day-like activity still echoing into my window from distant, more grown-up activities elsewhere—my brothers and sister sequestered themselves in private intellectual spaces and turned heavy pages. Like scientists and magnates (and my inconceivably grownup and important dad with his papers and folders in his briefcase), they were learned and important and in control.

Grade school years passed by with me anxiously anticipating the day that I would join them—no doubt—and be seen with *my* armload of important books striding home to the grave business of homework and adulthood. Well, it didn't quite work out the way that I had imagined it. Sometimes it doesn't seem like I got a fair shot at it. At least not until much later.

By fifth grade one could say that my best days as a student were behind me. The years before then were effortless and successful because—I suspect—of my sense of humor and my natural ability in the areas emphasized in pre-teen education. Art, music, reading, creative writing, simple and fairly non-competitive sports—all undertaken in the context of letting the child "blossom" worked out well for me. (As did cracking up the teacher.) Unfortunately, the privilege of carrying those hallmarks of adulthood and responsibility home coincides with the "real" business of educating kids. Math. Schedules. Deadlines. Gym class.

Mathematics stopped making sense with the advent of times tables and memorization. Math (not cool important stuff) got sent home—along with its cruel books and mocking mimeographs. Flash cards made their hideous debut in my life and stayed for many years, as did a succession of unsuccessful tutors and summer schools. At every juncture lay the opportunity to demonstrate that I could not remember what I had been taught a few moments before. Math gave me a chance during evenings, weekends, and summer breaks to chew the same bitter cud and roll the same boulder up the same unconquerable hill for the bulk of my pre-teen and early teen life. I can only wonder how fate discovered that math could only be made worse by putting it on a *schedule*.

"Now, children," the teacher would chirp, "put down your crayons and get out your times tables. It's time for arithmetic." But, my picture isn't done yet. I'm not done reading. My short story has no ending. I *hate* math. No one ever sent picture drawing assignments home for homework (although every incomplete, hastily-pulled-together, sloppy, incorrect book report, take-home quiz, and math project was turned in late with *lovely* illustrations and signed collage for a cover).

Soon I became expert at ducking for cover. Some say that there is no such person as The Invisible Man. Even the idea of being invisible seems preposterous to the rational mind. I don't agree. If I tried hard enough I was periodically able to become so small, to radiate so little presence in the classroom, that I could become invisible and go home having put off discovery by my adversary, the teacher, for one more day. If any one feeling remains palpable from those years of decline it is the feeling of putting off today the inescapable misery of tomorrow. The same lack of ability and preparation that I hid from view in class Monday would certainly—given the odds—necessitate a public airing when, on Tuesday, my lowered head, averted gaze, and still hand failed to prevent my being called on for a turn at the blackboard.

If there is a God, why didn't He prevent this humiliation? I did not *raise* my hand because I did not *know* the answer. Believe me, if by some miracle I knew what stupid 12 x 12 was I would have knocked other students over to get the teacher's attention.

My powers of invisibility failed me the worst in gym class. They make you take off your clothes—see how scrawny I am? They make you take the President's Physical Fitness Test in front of your classmates—watch me fail the *United States of America* everyone. We all get a chance to walk on a balance beam—perhaps I'll fall and crush my own skull, altogether less painful than wind-milling and klutzing off the beam at the two-foot mark. Rope climbing race, anyone? It's fun! See who gets to the bell first. Or, perhaps if I'm lucky, I'll get to stand in a firing squad and have a big kid whip a ball at my head in order to enrich my physical and mental development.

The gym teacher, "Mr. Pudarski," rarely waited for me to raise my hand to let him know that I was ready to participate in his regimented, rule-bound games. Instead, fittingly, we counted off. I could only hope that he would have us count off in prime numbers or by sevens. My utter lack of ability in gym *and* math would have then come full circle in front of one and all. A lousy student, a weakling, and a dummy.

October 9, 1975

Dear Philip,

Thank you for your letter and thank you for the misspelled words. There is a reason why I wanted the misspelled words. I have found that the children in my research project that have learning disabilities like yours had more trouble spelling phonetically than did the children with a different type of learning problem. It would seem likely that the way a person has been trained to spell would make a difference in his approach, though. It looks as though you spell fairly phonetically, but I can tell that your perceptual-motor problem interferes with both writing and spelling.

I think giving up soccer is probably a good idea, and I am glad you suggested it. In the first place, free time *is* important. In the second place, the therapy activities give you as much exercise as you need. In the third place, six months from now your coordination will be better and you will enjoy sports more. We are not always sure about helping with an academic problem, but almost all people improve in their coordination. It is kind of a spin-off from the therapy.

I am glad you like riding the scooter board. That means that your brain can process the sensory input from that activity. It worries me that you roll so much you get nauseated. Can't you roll slower or stop before you get that way? While you are on the scooter board turn around a few times in a circle in place of rolling. When you have balancing equipment, more time on the balancing should help reduce the nausea part.

The size of the platform swing may not be critical. The blue one in the film was commercially made and is larger than another that I also use. Maybe the larger one is easier. You can probably tell better than I can.

The Tip-and-Turn that my brother Richard designed would be good for you if you can manage it and tolerate it. I find it too difficult for most people and it doesn't take many turns to get a sensory overload. Sometimes people put their hands and knees on the platform and shift their body weight to make it turn. Shifting the weight would be good for you, for that's the thing that will help your brain to organize the vestibular input. Maybe you can get someone to help turn it as you, too, try to turn it.

Your dad writes that the leaves are at their best right now. I'm glad to hear that, for next year at this time Franklin and I may be visiting one of the scenes of his childhood—New Hampshire. I will be lecturing in Boston and set the time to fit the leaves, hopefully. Your dad says fall is a little early this year, but I would think it would be even earlier in New Hampshire, that should make the prediction about right.

I'll look forward to hearing from you next time, Phil. The letter doesn't need to be long—just tell me what feels good and what doesn't. Any misspelled words help me to get the picture better.

Love,
Jean

Where Can I Turn?

BY ZOE MAILLOUX

PARENTS KNOW THEIR CHILDREN better than anyone. When a parent feels that something is not right, they are usually correct. If the problem is obvious, like a hearing loss or weak muscles, it will usually not be difficult to find out what is wrong and to get the appropriate help. However, when the problem is hard to see or to name and if it is not commonly understood, a parent can flounder for a long time before being able to get the right kind of help.

When parents contact me they often say that they have been concerned about their child for a long time. It is common to hear that they have described their worries to many people and that no one has recognized what the problem might be. Often parents find help by chance. A neighbor might mention that their child is receiving help for difficulties that sound similar to the concerns a mother has about her own child. One mother told me that she typed random phrases such as "afraid of swings" in an Internet search and eventually found help. Unfortunately, I commonly hear that parents, particularly mothers, have been told that the problem most likely is the result of their parenting style. Overcoming feelings of guilt often becomes part of the discovery process for parents. Feelings of relief and validation are also common. I cannot count the number of times I have heard, "This is the first time someone has put words to the feelings I have had about what is going on with my child." My colleagues tell me that they hear similar comments.

While more and more teachers, psychologists, and doctors are recognizing sensory integration dysfunction, most professionals in these fields do not receive much training about these problems. The group of professionals who tend to have the most training in sensory integration theory and practice are occupational therapists. The basic principles of the theory, evaluation, and treatment associated with this approach are taught in all accredited occupational therapy programs. Physical therapists and speech and language pathologists are also likely to have received some basic training in sensory integration concepts. Although introductory information may be taught to the extent that most occupational therapists, many physical and speech and language therapists, and some teachers and psychologists and physicians will be familiar with sensory integration concepts, advanced training is required for a professional to be qualified to evaluate and treat sensory integrative disorders. Reputable therapists should feel comfortable being asked about the following standard qualifications:

A university degree and a license, registration, or credential in a recognized professional field such as occupational or physical therapy, speech and language pathology, psychology, education, or medicine. Sensory integration is an approach applied by these fields, but there is not a separate professional discipline of "sensory integration." Parents should beware of people who call themselves "sensory integration therapists," if they are not a validated member of one of the professions listed above.

Advanced, post-graduate training in specialized courses in sensory integration theory, evaluation and treatment. At least 30 hours of advanced study is usually expected. Therapists should be able to produce a certificate or other documentation of their advanced training.

Clinical experience of at least three to four months under the supervision of an experienced mentor. Therapists should be able to describe the extent of their clinical experience with regard to ages and diagnoses of individuals with whom they have worked.

Evidence of ongoing training, education, and experience. Sensory integration is an evolving theory that is updated as new research advances knowledge and influences evaluation and intervention choices. Therapists using this approach should be able to show evidence of ongoing, current learning experiences.

If you suspect that your child may have problems in sensory integration, you should mention your concerns to your child's pediatrician and/or teachers. These professionals may be familiar with these kinds of problems and be able to help you find resources in your community. Hearing your concerns will also give them an opportunity to share their impressions of your child. However, if they seem unaware of sensory integration dysfunction, or if they tell you to "wait and see," you will probably need to rely on other sources of help.

Finding an occupational therapist in your community with the qualifications listed above is a good place to start. To do this, contact your local pediatric hospital or school district and ask to speak to the occupational therapy department. Even if these agencies do not employ therapists with training in sensory integration, the therapists in those departments are likely to be familiar with the resources in the community.

October 22 1975

Dear Phil:

I was delighted to get your letter of October 19 and I found its contents most encouraging.

The fact that you can notice improvement in coordination as a result of the activities indicates that your nervous system can change in a positive direction. If it has changed that much in a few months, it will probably change some more in the coming months. I am particularly pleased with your report of reduced nausea when swinging on the platform swing. That means your brain is modulating the vestibular input better. As it becomes better modulated, you will be able to tolerate more movement; more movement will, in turn, help your nervous system to work better. It is like breaking a vicious circle.

Glad to hear the football device is working out well. I don't think I gave you very good directions for using it, but you seem to have done well with what I said. Here is a more explicit set of directions. The objective is to get your brain to send automatic messages to the muscles that make your trunk muscles contract just enough to keep your center of gravity on the ball. I suspect those automatic movements don't come through very automatically with you. You may have to help them by thinking about rotating your trunk a little and consciously doing it when you find yourself beginning to roll to one side, or bending your trunk if you start to go forward or backward. The best way to do that is to first position yourself on the ball so that you are close to being able to balance, then put one hand on the floor. Then try not to use your hand to help you balance, just to keep you from falling off, but try to balance by wiggling your trunk. If it doesn't come naturally, explore movements a little bit by deliberately moving your trunk one way or another to see the effect.

Another way of getting those reactions is by nailing a piece of wood about 2"x2" on the bottom of a larger piece of wood. Then get on top of the wood on your hands and knees and rock the board back and forth in different directions.

Something else you might try sometime is a jumping board. I don't use one because it is difficult to get one light enough for me to carry around but sturdy enough to hold up. Put a piece of 2x4 crosswise at either end of a long, narrow board that has a spring to it, then jump on it. Maybe a 2x6 would be better for a 14 year old.

Incidentally, many parents have reported growth spurts as a result of sensory integrative therapy. You might be interested in keeping track of your growth rate.

Blowing on a tin whistle while on the platform swing (which is mostly for balancing rather than swinging) is a good idea. The automatic system often comes in better if the consciousness is directed elsewhere.

Love,
Jean

Roman Holiday

BY PHILIP R. ERWIN

I SURVIVED THE FINAL MONTHS of my mid-year sixth grade placement. I don't remember much about those days. I don't think that there was much good about them to remember. When summer vacation arrived I faced the specter of summer school for the first of many times. The term "summer school" evokes some visceral emotions in me. I was transported into a non-summer, non-vacation place and force-fed the stuff I liked the least, day after day.

I spent the coolest, best part of the mornings alone with a very nice, very tall man who drove a Peugeot (pronounced "Piggot" by him). He ran the numbers with me. As always I retained what he wanted me to learn for a day or two. My math memory and conceptualization seems to function the way dreams do. You know, you wake up after a vivid dream and can still remember the plot. Then you try and remember it again and pieces of it start to elude you. They aren't part of your permanent memory, just a funny sort of housecleaning done by your brain while you rest. Your recollections are just the dust drifting away while your mind puts away the broom. Mr. Piggot relentlessly drilled me in the various arithmetic arts. I could follow his trail long enough—while it was still warm—to get through the summer term. By autumn, though, fallen leaves obscured a cold path. I would return to school—my first year of middle school—not knowing where I had been, what I had been doing, or where I was to going.

At least I made friends. I was able to establish myself using proven survival tactics: humor, art, and imagination. I D'd and F'd myself through math. I bluffed my way through deadlines and schedules. I fiddled around in science by playing with the microscopes.

I began to encounter a problem that would vex me for some time to come: group projects. The chance to participate and carry a share of responsibility for a group's success or failure depending on if you followed through or not is the hallmark of cooperative and competitive learning. The problem I had is that I loved to plan—the more grandiose the better. I loved to think up the most involved presentations possible. I, however, was unable to follow through, much as I might have liked to. I usually tried to find the managerial role. "I'll coordinate," I'd volunteer. That would go on long enough for the teacher to realize that I could only plan in the present. When I got home all efforts and all bets were off. The only thing that could make it worse was if there were some sort of physical challenge involved.

The Roman Holiday was an all-seventh grade gathering involving every class in which various "typically Roman" activities took place. I suggested that we build chariots. I could visualize the plan and set about drafting up complex pictures of a sleek, human powered racing machine. How hard could it be?

Harder than I thought, I suppose, seeing as how my suggestion was roundly (and wisely) voted down by the poor adults who would have had to salvage the effort had it gone forward.

We settled on a traditional Roman marathon, run in a tag-team format. I had two things going for me. First, I had the notion that running—of all things—could not be *that* hard. I ran *all the time*. So I volunteered for a key, very public leg—the anchorman. Second, I had time. Heck, the race wasn't for weeks. I could come up with a strategy in time—maybe even set a schedule and practice, you know, get in shape. Yep, stick to the plan.

The morning of the race I figured I had better come up with something. I thought about pleading that I broke my arm and couldn't run. No, that required too much from the prop department, and I had already had trouble with the authorities on the "faking injury" front before. The hour of the race approached. The best, most motivated student athletes—as well as me—lined up for the start. The first relay bolted. I had some time to figure things out now. The relay returned and tagged the second, and penultimate bunch, and off they went. I was on the line—waiting. Faint? No. Turn, run, and disappear? Uh-uh, I'd get caught before I got too far. Tag! Off I ran.

The first fifty feet at a full sprint weren't so bad. Then the pack moved off into the distance and made the turn. It was after they were already heading back my direction that I begin to limp. Yes, ol' reliable—the excuse—came through when ol' unreliable—me—couldn't. That darn "trick knee," or hip, or whatever, acted up just in time to prevent me from saving the day and bringing home the laurel. I'm sure everyone on the team understood how disappointed I was after all of the hyperbole and preparation I had invested. School broke for summer not long after I failed the Roman Empire. I was destined for a new school for eighth grade and had a summer of math ahead of me.

A. JEAN AYRES

TORRANCE, CA

November 12, 1975

Dear Philip:

I looked forward to your letter and enjoyed receiving it. I think about you often in between letters. I like to respond to them right away, but this time flu and an out-of-town trip interfered.

Yes, sensory integrative therapy can and does get tedious. I am glad you can think of ways of making it more interesting. Scooting after a ball that your mother rolls is not only good from an interest standpoint, but also helps eye-body coordination.

Here is something else that will vary the routine. Remember that what we want is accelerated movement of your head through space on every plane we can think of. That is why you push off from a wall. If you kept a constant speed for 30 seconds, the movement receptors would adjust and stop discharging. You can get pretty much the same sensory input and more times per minute by lying prone (stomach down) in the net hammock suspended from one overhead point and pushing yourself forward with your hands on the floor, then letting yourself swing backward. You can work up quite a swing that way. I try to get side-ways movement when boys are in the net by holding their feet and swaying them from side to side. I doubt if you can do that by yourself, but you might try. While the net gives more sensory input per minute than the scooter board, it does not demand quite so much of a motor response, and the motor response may be important in helping you to organize the input. When I am not altogether sure which of two activities is better, I suggest half the time be spent on each. So why don't you go to the church, which has long, smooth hallways, two or three times a week for scooter board work, and do the swinging in the net two or three times a week. This will give you variety and also flexibility for other demands that might be made on your mother or by weather.

While swinging in the net, you can make life more interesting by picking up beans from the floor and tossing them into a box. Also attracts mice. Also helps eye-hand coordination.

Certainly jumping on a mattress is just as effective as jumping on a board, and probably a lot more fun.

I've sent you by slow mail a large inflatable ball left over from the last project. It has been folded so long it may crack. You can do lots of patching with patching material. You may not be quite ready for this ball. Try it this way. Put just a little air in it, then lie on it keeping your hands and feet on the floor, but no more than necessary to keep you on the ball. The idea is to try to make your body change its position automatically so that it stays on the ball with minimal help from your hands. When you can do that add a little more air and try using overhead ropes as shown in the film. Don't let yourself fall on cement.

Love,
Jean

The Sensory Integration Approach to Therapy

BY ZOE MAILLOUX

ONE OF THE THINGS most confusing about having a child with sensory integrative dysfunction is that this terms applies to a diverse group of symptoms and patterns of difficulties. There are many types of sensory integration disorders, and the functional problems associated with them will vary from child to child. Recognizing that a child has dysfunction in sensory integration is a little like saying that a child has allergies. Some children are allergic to cats and sneeze when they are around them, while others might develop a rash as an allergic reaction to grass, and others still might be allergic to foods that cause a stomachache.

We understand that "allergies" is a broad term that describes a kind of problem that appears in different patterns. Some children might have allergies without having any other problems, while children with certain diagnoses, like asthma, might be more likely to have allergies in conjunction with that disorder. The same is true for sensory integration dysfunction. Some children will have signs of poor sensory integration without any other recognizable problem or diagnosis, while other children will have sensory integration dysfunction in conjunction with identifiable medical or educational disorders.

Some diagnoses are more commonly associated with dysfunction in sensory integration than others. Children with diagnoses related to poor attention and hyperactivity have been found likely to have sensory integration dysfunction, especially in a pattern characterized by heightened sensitivity to sound, touch, motion and other sensory experiences.

A learning disability is an example of an educational diagnosis that seems to overlap a great deal with problems in sensory integration. A common sensory integration dysfunction associated with problems in learning is inefficiency in the functions of the "vestibular" system, a little known, but extremely important sensory system that contributes to many aspects of learning. Some researchers have estimated that up to 50 percent of children with reading problems also have signs of poor vestibular function.

One of the most rapidly growing diagnoses in children is autism. This neurologically based disorder associated with unusual speech and language development, poor social skills, and atypical behavior patterns is also commonly associated with abnormalities in sensory and motor planning functions. Children with autism commonly have strengths in visual perception, but are more likely to show signs of atypical touch, movement or sound perception, poor body awareness, difficulty in motor planning and overall sensory responsiveness that is unusually under- or over-reactive.

There are a variety of less common or well-known diagnoses that tend to overlap with problems in sensory integration. In addition to neurologically or developmentally based disorders, environmentally induced conditions such as pre-natal drug exposure and sensory deprivation (such as that encountered by children in orphanages) also tend to have significant associations with sensory integration problems.

A. JEAN AYRES
TORRANCE, CA

November 19, 1975

Dear Phil:

Sounds as though your sensory integration is coming along all right. You are certainly doing all of the things that I know to do and putting in lots of time.

You are right to continue doing the scooter boarding if it might be making you feel happier. The vestibular system has a fairly direct connection to the septum, which is the pleasure center of the brain. Some of us suspect that the reason so many of the things most people find pleasurable, such as skiing, are pleasurable is because of the vestibular stimulation. There is also apparently a strong drive to get our bodies to learn to relate to gravity, and if that relationship isn't established, we tend to be uncomfortable.

Maybe someday you will want to check with Drs. Jan Frank and Harold Levinson. They practice in New York City (it may be Brooklyn), and I believe they are psychiatrists. They have published results of their study of what is called dyslexia (or trouble reading). They, like me, feel that the vestibular system is involved in learning disorders and treat the vestibular system with medication—something like Dramamine. They test the vestibular system by attaching metal plates around the eye muscles and the current from the muscles is recorded as an electronystagmagram. I have known of only one person who has had medication and he didn't tolerate it well, but Frank and Levinson report good results.

Their information is so well known you might want to ask your personal physician about it sometime. In any event, I don't think I would pursue that course of action until you get your vestibular system working as well as you can from natural activities such as you are doing now. Of course, if the occasion arises naturally to make it easy to investigate this approach, don't turn it down.

Phil, it looks to me as though your writing is reflecting better eye-hand coordination. If that is really the case, it is probably the exercises that have done it. Does that help any? I sure feel with you on those depressing days at school.

Love,
Jean

Gym Class

BY PHILIP R. ERWIN

DOES ANYONE REALLY LIKE physical education class? Well, I suppose some kids in junior high and senior high school tolerate it — or even (*harumph*) look forward to gym class. I couldn't tell you about that though because I cannot *imagine* feeling anything except revulsion at the thought of it. Anyhow, I so completely loathed that part of my education that I have a hard time seeing what anyone could have gotten from it.

I suppose you might ask me, "Hey what's the big deal, why so sore about sports, guy?"

I was small for my age.

I was terminally uncoordinated.

I had poor large motor control.

I had problems locating myself in three-dimensional space.

I had trouble tracking objects in motion in space (such as balls hurtling towards me).

The result was that when someone threw a ball at me I wouldn't be able to hit it or catch it (whatever your pleasure was at the moment), and would struggle merely to stay out of its way. I disliked these activities because they involved no imagination and my creative interpretation had no effect on their brutal, sweaty realities. Winning was never an option for me.

I've mentioned before the twin miseries of the President's Physical Fitness Exam and dodge ball, seventh grade's method of nationalizing my incompetence while enforcing my fear of moving objects. And while there were lots of naturally gifted jocks drinking up the chance to run around in sanctioned bullying venues, intimidating other kids at school, there was certainly another population at school who dreaded that period each and every time it came up. I felt intensely this way because I was neither a gifted athlete nor was I neurologically prepared for the rigors presented both physically and emotionally in typical physical education classes.

So I managed to muddle through junior high school gym classes by employing my proven survival strategy: be invisible; accept your inevitable loss as quickly as possible; and withdraw to the "out" bench and its temporary sanctuary until the class was over.

Modeling real life, things had to get a lot worse before they could begin to get better. Acting on bad advice and misleading advertising, Mom and Dad enrolled me in a private prep school for eighth and ninth grades. In those ivy-covered halls of pain there existed no gym class. Oh no. Instead of physical education class there was mandatory participation on the school's notoriously under-performing and losing athletic teams. But hey, I had *choices*!

In the autumn I could play soccer. In the winter I could choose to join either the basketball or ice hockey team. And, in the spring, I could choose to play baseball or lacrosse. With each of my choices I had to come up with unique survival strategies.

Soccer worked like this. First, try to be invisible on the bench and avoid playing at all. Since I had no understanding of the rules, principles, or fundamentals of the game, when the coach/ seventh grade English teacher would force me into the game I would rely upon his saying, "Go in and relieve so and so as right wing." That way I would know where to go and stand. Next, run towards the guy with the ball. Slide to the ground and try to kick the ball. Get up as the pack moves off. Raise hand to be removed from game. Repeat until successfully returned back to the bench. (What the heck is offsides anyway?)

In the winter I chose basketball over ice hockey for two reasons. First, I would have been killed out there. Second, I couldn't skate. In eighth grade I was five feet tall and weighed 65 pounds. We seemed to play against school teams where the guys shave at halftime and are cheered on by their wives and kids in the bleachers. I had no idea what was going on at any point of the practice or the game. The rules, the strategy, the point of it all? I had no idea whatsoever. It seems that *prima facie* knowledge is always assumed in young boys regarding sports. I disproved that assumption daily.

My basketball survival strategy was similar to soccer in that its foundation was avoidance. Avoid going into the game. Avoid staying in the game any longer than necessary (which for me was *one second*). As a rule, stay away from the ball and anyone who has it. Always keep someone between you and the guy who has the ball to avoid having the damnable object tossed at you. If the unthinkable happens and you end up with the ball—*get rid of it immediately*! Throw it to someone else, do a hopeless airball shot at the basket, or get it taken away by a big guy from the other team. (The latter was usually my move.) Having proven my inability in public for a sufficient length of time, I'd raise my hand to be relieved. Repeat until successful and slink back to the sanctuary of the bench.

Ah, Spring! A time when young men's minds focus on the good ol' field of dreams. Yep, get out there and throw the ol' pill around and have the good ol' pill whipped at your face at ninety miles an hour by an out of control 15-year-old. Mmmm, I can hear the cheers now: "Hey batta, whiffer batta, whiffer, whiffer, whiffer." Yeah, I "chose" baseball over lacrosse because I wanted to live to see 14.

Now negotiating baseball requires some real skill. First, you must try to stay off of the roster—not easy in the egalitarian society that is junior high school team sports. If forced to bat, *stand still.* Maybe the pitcher won't hit you if you leave him infinite amounts of space surrounding you in which to rifle the baseball. Ironically, by just standing there one was not certain of the outcome. I mastered the standing still strikeout, the standing still walk, and the standing still hit-by-the-pitch, take-your-base maneuvers.

Way out in right field—the best the coach could do to mitigate the risk of involving me in his march to victory—I found God. I prayed continually. Please, oh please do not let that ball come out here. Amen. I learned a lot about religion and the power of prayer on the field of dreams.

The crack of the bat, the ball "fffffffiff-ing" across the dry spring grass towards me, the coach, the team, yelling at me.

The ball going past me and me running after it and finally throwing my glove at it to stop it.

The throw. Accurate within a forty-degree arc and good for but a quarter of the necessary distance.

Somewhere towards the noise.

Somewhere over there. Away. Amen.

I fear not death because team sports allowed me to experience spiritual and emotional death every day for that year I was forced to participate in team sports. Nothing, I felt, could be worse. The next year I was placed in permanent study hall all afternoon until Mom picked me up to go and do Jeanie's therapy. I was saved!

After I was moved to the public high school and into special education, I had an entire team of teachers, counselors, and advocates setting me up in success-oriented educational and vocational situations. My papers were in order. I was documented.

Yet, the gym demon would not let go. No matter what, it was determined to make me participate in physical education. It was required and suppposedly for my own good. No gym; no graduation. So, new to yet another new school, in tenth grade I was enrolled in *coed gym*!

My coach was the women's volleyball-trix. The class was coed dancing. I was one of two guys in the class and the girls found me revolting (because I was). And I'm thinking, "I'm 15, a geek, can't dance and don't want to, and I'm already afraid of girls. What the heck are you people *thinking* putting me in this class?"

I dealt with it for a few weeks, but as ballroom dancing (left, left, right, left) transitioned into the high art of square dancing (memorized, geometrical, coordinated misery) I began getting myself thrown out of class. I'd feign mental breakdown. I'd mimic the teacher. I'd invent spaz-dance routines. I'd insist upon dancing with the other guy (after all, the girls got to dance with each other).

That was fall. In the winter I had the same coach. But the class was volleyball! And the class was composed entirely of her women's volleyball team! Thus I was presented with a golden opportunity both to suck and to be drubbed by cute girl athletes who detested me.

I'd had about enough of this crap and of the state's educational requirements. I skipped the last two-thirds of that term's gym class—and nobody could make me go. I was ready to walk out on the whole high school experience at that point.

Enter Bob May. He was my mentor for all of my Special Education internships (where my real education was taking place). Bob realized that we were at an impasse. They could push, but I was done yielding. *NO MORE GYM.*

Bob got me into "special gym."

There were five or six of us in special gym. There was Andy, who looked about 40 and drove a bulldozer for a living even though he was only a nineteen-year-old senior in high school. There was Craig, a violent greaser whom I knew from the firehouse. He drove dump trucks and treated me all right. Tony was a weasely guy covered in tattoos. And there were others. The dirty half dozen. Lost gym causes given one last chance.

Bob took us bowling at the Westport Lanes. The place was always quiet when we arrived—perhaps a few women's league bowlers brunching at the scoring tables. Quiet until Andy or Craig would grab a ball and heave it across *the width* of the lanes. Bob would just sit and smile while all manner of harmless mayhem ensued.

The next year all of my special gym co-incarcerees graduated or disappeared. As I was a year away from graduating, I was still being held to the state's gym requirement. Once again Bob stepped in and arranged for me to do a new kind of special gym. There was a new gym teacher at the school: the gymnastics coach. She was actually very nice. Bob and she arranged for me to spend my last year of high school gym playing badminton with a kid who had suffered a stroke and lost the use of half of his body.

We'd meet in a small, unused section of the gym and just volley the shuttlecock back and forth. No one got hurt. No one lost. In fact, we both won. I showed up. The other kid got to play sports. We both graduated.

December 4, 1975

Dear Philip,

The equipment that you and your family made using two inner tubes is excellent and I commend all of you. I have used one inner tube as you illustrated, but it is hard to balance on only one. Using two makes it easy. This is what is good about it: it gives you the opportunity of not only swinging back and forth but also going around. Unlike a scooter board, it will also let you lie on your back and on your side. Try to swing getting your head in as many different positions as possible. The objective is to activate as many different receptors of the vestibular system as possible in order to get input over every aspect of the brain that is involved in the vestibular system. Some vestibular receptors respond to movement or position of one type and others to a different position or movement. Another good thing about this apparatus is that you have to contract the extensor muscles of your neck, back and legs. Theoretically, that muscle contraction elicits sensory input from the muscle receptors that enter the brain and helps modulate the vestibular input. Hopefully that will help to reduce the discomfort you experience from the vestibular stimulation, but I should think it almost normal to become nauseated after 25 minutes of swinging. (I swung in a dual swing with a child yesterday for about 10 minutes and felt queasy.)

The fact that you feel better in some respects (but not others) when you get the vestibular input tells us that it is helping your brain to be better integrated, at least for a while. The fact that your writing has improved so much says that your brain is better integrated on a more prolonged basis. Let's hope that you can continue in the direction that you are going.

I sure feel with you about these bad days at school. This may be one of those periods that teen-agers go through during sensory integrative therapy. Younger children don't seem to have these periods or they are less noticeable to us, but every teen-ager I know who has had sensory integrative therapy has disliked it and did it only because he needed to go. It takes a lot of will power to keep going when you are going through these difficult periods. I don't suppose this will be the last one, either, but there will be some "let-ups" in between. One 15-year-old whom my research assistant treated went through terrible periods, expressed by stealing and other anti-social behavior, and resisted therapy like mad. At the end of about 9 months therapy, when he was quitting, he said to the therapist, "It's kind of sad seeing this come to an end, isn't it?"

You certainly draw well, Phil; you always have been good at expressing form and space. Franklin noticed that you don't seem to be misspelling words the way you did earlier. Hope you're not looking them up for us.

Love,
Jean

Identifying and Understanding the Problem

BY ZOE MAILLOUX

PROFESSIONALS WITH EXPERTISE in sensory integration theory and practice always hope to identify problems at the youngest age possible. This is because sensory integration dysfunction is related to the way the child's nervous system processes information. We know that the development and function of young nervous systems can be influenced more significantly than older ones. The parts of the brain that take in sensory information and allow a person to respond to it undergo rapid and active development during infancy and early childhood.

We know that some children are deprived of important early sensory experiences, such as touch and movement, when they are in unfavorable environments like crowded orphanages or conditions of poverty that lack opportunities for play and positive social contact. Studies of animals in deprived or unfavorable sensory conditions have also shown that atypical development occurs in these situations. On the other hand, improving the sensory opportunities in the environment has a positive effect on the development of children (or animals) in these conditions. This research, as well as studies which have shown that the brain is malleable in early development, provides the foundation for emphasizing early intervention with sensory integration dysfunction whenever possible.

If a problem with sensory integration is suspected early, i.e. in infancy or in the preschool years, a therapist will rely on qualitative observations of the child's responses to sensation and performance of various motor skills. Once a child is four years of age, standardized tests are available for comprehensive evaluation of sensory integration functions. Dr. Ayres began developing tests in the 1950s and 1960s that evolved into a set of tests now called the Sensory Integration and Praxis Tests, abbreviated as the SIPT. Administering the SIPT requires specialized training and a therapist should be able to provide evidence of certification in using the SIPT, when asked.

The SIPT are designed to measure functions such as how well the child can perceive and interpret information from the senses that tell them what they see, what they feel through touch, how their bodies are positioned, and how they are moving through space. Abilities such as balancing on one foot, using both hands together, imitating actions, performing a series of movements, and following verbal directions to complete actions are also tested. When a child is given the SIPT, additional information is collected through parent (and often teacher) interviews and through observation of the child. Taken together, the standardized tests, observations, and interview information provide a comprehensive assessment of the child's sensory integration functions and allow the trained therapist to determine if a problem exists and whether or not intervention is warranted.

December 19, 1975

Dear Philip:

I'm mad at your school. They just don't understand neurological problems. But then, I guess they don't advertise that they do. I'll be glad when you can go to a different one. I don't blame you for not wanting to go away to school—a boarding school. If I were you I think I would want the comfort of your understanding and loving parents every night. I think I would rather go to one of the nearby schools that are for the emotionally disturbed, providing they had a fairly good idea about learning disabilities. Whether the people who run those schools know it or not, at least half of their students have some neurological problem. You might have to put up with observing some pretty ill behavior, but then, I think you might be able to offer them empathy. You know how it feels to be frustrated and misunderstood. Maybe even public schools plus private tutoring would be worth considering.

Phil, I can't be sure about the connection between your being especially upset these days and the therapeutic activities. I do know that most teen-agers do go through something like this. Younger children don't seem to, but they also don't get as much frustration from the school situation. You are getting enough there to account for your feelings about yourself. Considering the kind of nervous system you have to cope with, Phil, you really are doing pretty well with coping with life. I bet you can understand why so many boys with learning disabilities become juvenile delinquents. In fact, it is now thought that many or perhaps even most juvenile delinquents have irregular nervous systems.

A few years ago a couple of Australians took a course from me, then instituted many of my theoretical procedures into their clinic for learning disabled children. Another person associated with that clinic spent the other afternoon with me. He said that some of the children who got sick easily during vestibular stimulation took the medication that Frank and Levinson recommended and that enabled them to tolerate a great deal of spinning. My question to him was, "Does the medication do anything to prevent or reduce the effectiveness of the sensory stimuli?" He didn't know, of course, and I don't either, but it would be worth trying. How about getting some Dramamine or any other seasickness pills (no Rx needed) and taking them before you spin or swing? If you feel just as good after exercising with medication as you do without it, it might be worth your while to use it for a week and see if your tolerance or ability to modulate the input improves.

Love,
Jean

Shrinking Away

BY PHILIP R. ERWIN

MY PARENTS STARTED taking me to psychologists when I was ten or eleven years old. Despite that, I ended up being OK.

If I were to generalize about the psychological and psychiatric professions (an evil little pleasure) based on my experiences with the two psychologists and one psychiatrist to whom I was sent by Mom and Dad, I would say this: First, a majority of psychologists must themselves be in need of psychological help. Second, the primary focus of the psychologist is to create a "fan base" or a "following" in their quest for moderate wealth and local celebrity. And third, this metaphor:

> Sometimes when digging for gold
> A fisherman may walk into your camp
> And offer you fresh asparagus.

That is, occasionally one's efforts yield only collateral and unanticipated positive results.

I was beginning to stall out at school. I lit the family piano on fire the first time I was left home alone (and no, white correction fluid will *not* cover fire damage to white ivory). Of course there was the time I wrapped myself in ace bandages and convinced the teacher that I had third degree burns, yielding an unexpected and unpleasant visit to the principal's office to meet with my mom. All of this associated with my withdrawal into myself and my perpetual blue mood motivated my parents to seek more mainstream solutions.

Enter the three shrinks.

Dr. Nutty, who was recommended by my pediatrician, was the first. His little chamber of horrors was in the basement of a cheesy split-level ranch house across town. Windowless and banked low with smoke from his ever-present smoldering cigarettes, the room remains orange and close in my memory. After a limp, clammy handshake, I would sit across from this short, fat, bearded chain-smoker and—while he bit his nails to the quick—answer his questions and do his word associations. I remember wanting things to get better. The strange thing is I had no real idea—no better than those around me—of what was wrong. I didn't even really know how I felt. I was counting on my pal, Dr. Nutty, to explain my feelings to me, to tell me what was wrong, to validate some of my emotions, and most important, *to give me a solution.* I needed Dr. Nutty to save me—to tell me that I was all right and the world was wrong.

What my parents and I got was the diagnosis that my problems were rooted in the fact that my parents *spoiled* me.

Dr. Nutty told Mom and Dad that because they tucked their kid into bed at night, and let the kid's dog sleep on the bed, and that they felt that the kid's behavioral difficulties warranted investigation, my parents were coddling me. And they needed to break the cycle by sending that little kid—me—off to a boarding school. Perhaps a good military school would do the trick. Yep. That'll do it. Take a lonely, introverted kid and fix him up by separating him from his support network.

Mom and Dad sensed that Dr. Nutty had missed some

important points. They discontinued our relationship with him.

Next up was a psychiatrist, Dr. Star. I don't really remember much about what he did. I do remember that he was an example of Plato's perfect forms. Dr. Star looked like a psychiatrist. He wore white coats over tweed. He wore round, tortoiseshell glasses and had a salt-and-pepper beard and mustache. He was tall and scary. He spoke in kind tones and mouthed uncle-like compassion. But he exuded distance, coldness, and clinical cynicism. He was a local celebrity—in this wealthy little hamlet, everyone's kid went to Dr. Star when they began acting up. And Dr. Star would open their hoods, wrench around a little, and send the kids off ready to twist their parents' world into a knot as they roared into adolescence.

His diagnosis? I was immature, lazy, and spoiled. Thanks so much Dr. Star. Oddly enough, you didn't enhance your image as a celebrated local mind mechanic on me, and I ended up getting along with my parents despite the fact that I entered adolescence in distress.

Around this time, while driving to visit Grandmother's in Visalia, Mom lamented to Jeanie about the trouble Dad and she were having getting me fixed, and told her about the mess that the psychologists were making of everything. As Mom tells it, Jeanie gave her... *The Look.*

My guess is that *The Look* was an unspoken expression of several feelings. First, Jeanie had not interfered in my mom's parenting. Second, Jeanie had not had great experiences with psychologists of that era regarding acceptance of her work. And third—and I'm only guessing here—Jeanie probably felt some disappointment at the fact that she knew what was wrong with me and could fix it, but that we now lived 3000 miles away.

The problem was neither psychological nor psychiatric, of course. Instead, I had sensory integrative dysfunction. My vestibular system was out of whack. Psychology only came into it when I accounted for the socialization damage, the emotional destruction, and the depression and hopelessness that emanated from the hostility I felt from the sensible world.

Mom's older sister assured her that help had arrived and the therapies she had developed would probably help me—even though I was far older than those who typically would and should undertake therapy for sensory processing issues.

Now this wasn't the end of my contact with psychologists. It was the end of my dependence on conventional wisdom. In the course of diagnosing my sensory integration problems, Mom and Dad needed to find out if there were contributing factors to my problems.

We went to a psychologist whose office was about 45 minutes from home. The experiences with Dr. Meek stood in marked contrast to those who preceded them. Dr. Meek's office was quiet. Dr. Meek was quiet. He began each session by taking my radial pulse for five minutes. He was not concerned so much with the speed of my heart as he was with the quality of the systems that controlled it.

After gut-churning blood tests and glucose tests and allergy tests, Dr. Meek diagnosed me with borderline hypoglycemia. He put me on a radically restricted diet—no sugar, no wheat, no nuthin'.

In truth, long term, nothing Dr. Meek did helped me directly. I slowly reintroduced most foods into my diet. But, Dr. Meek had shown me that I could ameliorate some of my mood swings by controlling what I ate. Dr. Meek also embodied the gentle nature of a person committed to wellness in others from a personally healthy and happy standpoint.

In the end, sensory integration therapy, special education support, and personal validation from my family, teachers, and friends were the protocol that built the positive upon the positive, put the negative into context and made it survivable, and offered boundless points of opportunity that have seen me through to this day.

December 23, 1975

Dear Nancy:

Franklin and I so very much enjoyed your Christmas letter and card. Your wishes were very appropriate. Actually, I will probably see Franklin even less this year, for he will likely be at a test site a good part of the time.

I am glad Phil likes to ride the scooter board. I hesitated to say so, but it looks to me as though his learning problem may be tied up with this tonic labyrinthine reflex, too. I find that when I sit at my desk for a few hours, my muscles get tight and a few rides down the walk on the scooter makes me feel a lot better for a while.

If you would want to try coping with reading some pretty technical material, I will send you a copy of my book. It presumes considerable knowledge about neurology.

I recently did some lecturing in the Los Angeles City Schools. My perspective is widening. As I was leaving one school ground I was threatened by a boy with a vicious weapon. I just called him "honey" and he let me go with the equipment he wanted. The next day I had two escorts to my car.

Love to all,
Jean

Will My Child Be OK?

BY ZOE MAILLOUX

SOME OF THE COMMON QUESTIONS parents ask when they find out that their child has sensory integration dysfunction are, "Will it go away?" "Will he grow out of it?" "Will therapy cure the problem?" and similar questions that ultimately ask what the future holds. In reality, all parents worry about their children's future, knowing that accidents, drug abuse, or simply making poor choices can mean the difference between a bright and a bleak existence. However, parents of children with dysfunction in sensory integration are right to be concerned about how this "invisible problem" might limit their children's potential.

When a parent seeks and finds help for their child's sensory integration problems, I always feel that half the battle has been won. Clearly one of the most debilitating aspects of these disorders is the fact that they are little known and largely misunderstood. Whenever possible, helping the child to understand what is going on in his nervous system seems to be a positive step. The most common emotion I encounter from both parents and children upon learning about sensory integration dysfunction is relief. A great burden is lifted and there is often a sense of validation when there is a name for a previously confusing and vague condition. In addition, feelings of guilt are commonly alleviated, since parents and children alike often feel at fault for the problem. Well-informed and astute parents help their children a great deal as they learn to recognize how problems in sensory integration function are affecting learning, behavior, skill development, and social interactions.

Dysfunction in sensory integration is often referred to as a type of "inefficiency" of processes that occur in the brain and nervous system. Sensory integration functions typically occur automatically, fluidly, and subconsciously for most people. Some parents become alarmed to think that there might be a problem in their child's brain. However, sensory integration difficulties are not like the problems usually associated with "brain damage" or trauma. In most cases, the structures of the brain and nervous system are probably intact. It is more likely that the "messages" sent from one part of the brain and nervous system to another are not as clear, fast, or complete as expected.

One thing that is well documented about the structures and functions of the brain and nervous system is that they are "changeable," especially in a young person. The word "plastic" or "plasticity" is used to describe this characteristic of the brain. The fact that the brain is plastic allows us to be affected by the experiences we have, especially in early development, in both potentially positive and negative ways. We talked earlier about children whose development was affected by conditions of deprivation (such as in crowded orphanages) and that these children can make great gains when given more optimal developmental opportunities. The same principle is at work for children with dysfunction in sensory integration. They will often need individualized opportunities for experiences that will help their brains and nervous systems send and interpret messages more efficiently.

As important as sensory integration function is, it is still only part of what determines our success or failure in life. Intelligence, personality, drive, temperament, and persistence are all characteristics that will play an important role in whether or not any individual leads a satisfying and productive life. The most important thing a parent can do for a child with a sensory integration disorder is to ensure that this problem does not interfere with that process. This is accomplished by a combination of intervention and understanding.

January 1, 1976

Happy New Year, Philip!

Mighty fancy printing you did on your last letter. Interesting pen.

I would think that 15 minutes daily of exercise would keep you from losing what you have gained by way of improved neurological functioning and 30 minutes a day would keep you advancing slowly. One needs to let up once in a while, doesn't one?

Thank goodness for school vacations. They meant as much to me at your age as they do to you. It shouldn't be that way, should it?

Maybe I reacted too quickly and emotionally to your suggesting going to a boarding school. You might miss your folks, but what a relief it would be to at least have school be bearable. I don't find East Hadem on my map. Near what larger city is it and how far is it from Weston? There would be something comfortable about being with others who also have learning problems and probably to a lesser extent than you have. You probably would be asked by some of the other students to help them with their reading, since that is where learning problems most often interfere.

You know how I am going to spend New Year's Day? I'm to go over the test results (of the kind the occupational therapist gave you) of tests given by various therapists to children of various kinds of neurological disorders, especially learning disorders. I'm supposed to see if they have interpreted the results accurately. It's a pretty difficult job, both to detect the problem and determine whether or not it was detected accurately. We have a lot yet to learn about learning disorders. Meantime, people like you have suffered from the lack of knowledge among professionals.

Best to you and all your family.

Love,
Jean

Therapy Begins

BY PHILIP R. ERWIN

MOM AND DAD ASKED ME to spin in circles on a swing that Dad rigged up in the basement. I did not then, nor do I now, like to spin in circles. It upsets my stomach. But, spin I did. They checked my eyes after they abruptly stopped my spin. Corbin, my little brother, was down there with us and was spinning as well. What was funny is that our eyes did different things when we stopped spinning. Corbin was cracking my parents up by exaggerating the back and forth ticking movements of the eyes that is the normal neurological response. (They finally made him go upstairs when he kept forcing the issue.) I, on the other hand, had GI Joe eyes. The only movement in me was in my gut after repeating the process a few too many times.

In 1975, I was 14 years old. I was between eighth and ninth grade at the private prep school, making the transition from one disappointing year into another one just like it. Mom had been corresponding with Jeanie who advised her to have me evaluated by an occupational therapist. Jeanie suspected from descriptions of me by my mom that my learning and emotional problems were caused by an out of whack vestibular system. We went to a very nice private school in New York City, the Churchill School, during the summer and met with the therapist, Mrs. Petroni.

What I remember about taking the tests is that they took most of the day. I was hoping it would be discovered that I was an undiagnosed genius or had a secret power like x-ray vision or telekinesis. Unfortunately neither scenario bore out. However, I was found to have substantial problems with sensory integration. I didn't realize it at the time but, secret powers or not, a life-changing event had just occurred.

Jeanie sent literature, an 8-millimeter movie, directions, and a copy of her first book (*Sensory Integration and Learning Disorders,* Los Angeles: Western Psychological Services, 1973) to mom. She wrote that she felt badly because she couldn't be with us to direct my therapy. We agreed that Jeanie and I would write to each other every other week and that I would begin spinning, rolling on large beach balls, rocking on toy horses, and flying across the floor on my stomach on a scooter board. Jeanie periodically asked me to write to her (without me first correcting my errors) and to send examples of my completed homework. I often wrote to tell her how much I detested everything about school. She commiserated with me and revealed that her husband Franklin took offense on my behalf as well. I still can touch those times in my memory and remember how special it felt to have a private relationship with this beloved, wise person.

I didn't really understand that she was in the process of saving my life.

I still feel bad about the way I treated my mom during the 20-minute drive to the church basement where I undertook the therapy. I was in mandatory study hall for the bulk of every afternoon (while the rest of the school was on the playing field). Mom would pick me up at the front gate in the family's orange

Mazda station wagon. I don't know if I can describe what I felt like those afternoons, but I'll try.

I was furious.

I was tired of being bothered.

The daily humiliations, intrusions, manipulations, misunderstandings, and my feelings of indignation had reached their zenith.

I wanted to be left alone.

Once in the car I would unload all of this on my mom while she quietly drove to the church. I don't think she said much because she knew that I was inconsolable. Commentary, invited or otherwise, only pissed me off more. Being taken to roll around on the floor pissed me off. Being pissed off pissed me off. It must have been awful for her. Every afternoon. For weeks. For months. For years.

The church was quiet and abandoned at 3:00 in the afternoon. The basement had long, dark hallways that gradually curved in a "U" shape. I would get on the purple-carpeted scooter board—often against my will—and begin pushing off the walls and zigzagging down the hall. In a few minutes I would begin playing one of my games. I'd invented imaginary sporting events in which—unlike those at school at which I sucked—I was the master. I would push faster and glide farther. Soon my imagination was on its own, I was feeling better—good even. At some point I would scoot over to my mom and talk a bit. For her, it must have been like seeing the Wolfman or Mr. Hyde return to a human form.

After an hour or so we would get back in the car and head home. I felt different. The world felt like it had backed off of me. I felt supple. I would go for a walk with my dog most afternoons. After starting therapy, I was able to think about my situation from a position of moderation instead of from the point of view of a fugitive holding self-destruction as a viable final alternative.

January 14, 1976

Dear Phil:

You have done some more lovely printing with that interesting pen. I like the new game you and your mother have devised. Your program sounds good. I will be interested to know if you have tried the Dramamine and if you can spin in the hammock without getting dizzy when under its influence.

I am certainly glad to hear you are feeling happier. It may be that you have gone through the kind of distressing period I have mentioned, but I can't be sure. I suspect that you will have ups and downs for a number of years. As long as you are in a stressful academic situation you are bound to have unhappy periods.

Last summer when a friend of ours and her son were visiting in this area, she asked me to check her 3-year-old son whom the teachers said was having trouble balancing. He was reluctant to do many of the tasks I wanted him to do, so I didn't do a very good evaluation. I could not find anything especially wrong with his coordination.

Just after New Year's (Franklin and I both avoid Christmas), Franklin and I visited our friend for a day and a half. In his own home the boy did have a lot more things and I could see that he does, indeed, have a mild neurological problem which interferes with his coordination. His fingers are so jerky he can't draw without making wobbly lines. As a result he avoids drawing. It makes me feel sad, of course, because here is a boy with inferiority feelings and he isn't even 4 years old.

His mother was so concerned about doing everything just right to help him be born perfect so he wouldn't have any problems. Not everything worked out well, though. He was weeks late in being born and was delivered by Caesarean section. I don't know if that is what caused it, though. I see a lot of children with that kind of coordination problem. I don't think it is going to interfere with his learning, for it isn't that type of problem. It's motor, not sensory. But it has already interfered with his personality development. I am beginning to think that not very many people get through the first week of post-natal life with all of their neurons working well. And there are more and more people who don't. Our friend's son also has a very inconvenient gastro-intestinal problem. I wonder if what went wrong didn't also make that problem.

Love,
Jean

Aren't They Just Playing?

BY ZOE MAILLOUX

ADDRESSING DYSFUNCTION in sensory integration is usually accomplished with a combination of three types of solutions. One way of coping with these kinds of problems is to develop strategies for compensating for the disorder.

An example of this might be seen in a child who is unable to learn to tie his shoes due to poor motor planning and visual perception skills. A strategy to compensate for the problem is to only purchase shoes without shoelaces. This helps the child to get by for a while and may offer relief from that specific burden, but the strategy would probably need to be adjusted to meet the challenge differently in the future.

Another way to address the problem is to develop a structured way to perform a specific skill and to practice it over and over until it becomes automatic. We can probably teach a child to tie shoelaces with enough practice, but the same child might need additional practice to tie a bow on a different pair of shoes, and may not be able to tie a bow on gift box at all. Therefore, this approach may offer an immediate practical solution, but may not offer solutions to other situations.

A third approach is to provide therapy that improves the basic underlying functions so that the actual problem is diminished. Improving function is the primary focus of therapy using a sensory integration framework.

Therapy aimed at improving basic functions of the brain and nervous system is possible because of the characteristic of "plasticity," or changeability, of these structures, especially before they are fully matured. Just as children develop abilities and capabilities through their regular developmental experiences, having the *opportunity* for certain kinds of challenges and activities can also influence their development. A paradox of this approach is that it is a complex process that requires years of specialized training and study, yet if provided appropriately *it looks like play*.

There is no set protocol or prescribed regimen for therapy aimed at improving sensory integration function. In this way, it is a little like parenting. Each child is different and thus requires different interactions. There really is no set recipe or answer for how to be a parent. Parents who know their children well learn to read their "signs and signals" and know what things will help their children respond, behave, and learn best.

It is similar for therapists. Armed with the knowledge of how the nervous system responds and develops functions, the therapist strives to know each child in a way that allows effective selection of activities chosen just for that child. Because a child who is having fun is likely to be more motivated and to persist even when things become challenging, a playful atmosphere is a characteristic of this type of therapy. In addition, therapy aimed at improving sensory integration function typically provides the types of experiences that a child is naturally driven to seek, but may not be able to engage in without help and support.

The feelings of satisfaction and pleasure from successful participation in these meaningful activities can make a child feel happy, organized, and complete. I have heard many children say things like, "I never want to leave this place," or "I wish therapy would never end."

A. JEAN AYRES
TORRANCE, CA

January 28, 1976

Dear Phil:

Thank you for experimenting with the Dramamine. Am I correct in interpreting your message to the effect that it helps when you are swinging back and forth in one plane for a minute? Don't feel that you need to keep taking the Dramamine if you would rather not, and I wouldn't take any more than is absolutely necessary. We don't know whether it will keep the movement from doing what we want it to do. Remember that when you can't do anything else by way of therapy, you can always roll on the floor. That's one of the best things to do, anyway.

I will be interested to know what your reaction is to the public school in Weston.

Phil, I hope that you can remember just what it is about academic work that is hard and what helps, for someday you may be teaching kids just like yourself.

Maybe you better not tell your mom this; it might make her green with envy. We have had the most beautiful January you can imagine. The temperature in downtown L.A. has been in the 80s ever so many days, but here nearer the beach, it has been cooler— perhaps in the high 70s. And sun every day. Would that June would be as lovely. The high school girl who cleans for me was lamenting today that beach weather and beach season just don't coincide. She was also too hot while cleaning mats for me outside today. Of course, what we really need is rain.

Have you heard of the malpractice insurance problem in

California? Rates for physicians have gone up 300 to 400%. The company which insured me as a psychologist discontinued offering malpractice insurance and the new company won't include bodily injury in its coverage. An insurance agent cannot find a company that will insure me, so I am preparing a form for parents to sign that will state that they will not hold me responsible for injury to their children. You can see why I need that, can't you.

Do you have a between-semester break? Do you think you will stick it out at your current school for the rest of the year? It's comforting to me to know that you will likely be making some kind of change, sometime.

Best,
Jean

Magical Footwear

BY PHILIP R. ERWIN

CHANGE DID NOT OCCUR OVERNIGHT. Instead I was transformed in several ways over several months. Previously I had viscerally disliked balancing and climbing on things. I spent most of my free time in non-physical, non-competitive activities and private games of imagination. Solitude was fine with me.

One day I got new sneakers. It had been a very snowy winter, meaning that I couldn't spend much time out of doors. One day it thawed and I went outside to play. I picked up my long-unused lacrosse stick and used it to toss a tennis ball against the garage door. To my utter amazement and elation *I actually caught it!*

I then felt an overwhelming urge to climb the big tree in the backyard. I clambered up it with ease. Great shoes, I thought.

But then I felt an urgent need to climb every tree on the large property where I walked my dog. I needed to get on the roof of the garage. I felt compelled to swing and climb on the structures at the playground at the school in back of our house. I needed to ride my bike. For the first time in my life I felt as if I had a *physical* presence on the planet. For the first time in my life I didn't feel puny. We were well beyond good footwear. Something inside me was changing.

My final year at the prep school was dismal. At every turn I was presented with evidence that I was substandard and a misfit. But my skills at coping effectively with these assaults were bolstered, I believe, by two things. First, I had been reassured that my failure to thrive in the school was not entirely my fault and was not necessarily my only destiny: hope was evident. Second, I felt better about myself because the therapies I was receiving were enabling me to cope with all of the stimulation—good and bad—in a more organized fashion. The world had gradually become a less hostile place for me. And great changes were on the horizon.

February 20, 1976

Dear Philip,

Sure is good to hear that you have a few moments of feeling great now and then. The fact that you feel so good after your scooter boarding at the church says that the sensory input you get there is just what your brain needs.

I am not sure I am interpreting "tunneling" properly, but I guess it is a matter of going back and forth between walls, changing direction every few seconds. If that is what it is, it is very good. The greatest sensory input comes during the period of sudden, rapid acceleration and deceleration. At a constant speed, the sensory receptors adapt and stop discharging. You must be getting a lot of very strong sensory input that your brain is able to modulate, perhaps because of the sensory input coming in from the neck muscles.

I wish I could think of something to make it more interesting, but it looks as though you and your mom are better at that than I am.

I like the idea of a 540-degree spin. That must be just the right amount of rotation—not so much as to make you sick, but enough to give you some good sensory input from the semicircular canals.

Have you noticed, Phil, that when you feel good your writing is also good and the letters are all even and consistent, but when you don't feel good your coordination is also less good? That suggests that the same thing that is making your coordination poor or math difficult also makes you feel depressed.

The camp sounds great. I am glad you have chosen to be tutored in English. All of us need English in any job that we do, but all most of us need in math are a few concepts and a calculator.

You are correct about the things you are doing being fun for others. It would take quite a bit of enginuity (that's not spelled right) to figure out ways of having a group be involved in those activities without a lot of equipment.

It would be helpful to you to continue the therapy while you are in camp, but if it is not feasible, I wouldn't worry too much about it. You will probably have a lot of other motor activity that will help you to keep what you have gained, and you might be able to figure out some way of getting some back-and-forth or spinning movement in while there without equipment. Of course, it would be best if all of the L.D.s [learning disabled] could be doing what you are doing.

Guess where I am going this afternoon to lecture Saturday and Sunday? Moraga! Your mom and dad will remember Moraga.

Love,
Jean

How Will I Know if Therapy Is Helping My Child?

BY ZOE MAILLOUX

SINCE THE MAIN FOCUS of therapy using a sensory integration approach is to change and to influence the development of basic neurological functions, progress is not usually immediately evident. However, sensory experiences can be powerful and sometimes children will demonstrate noticeable changes during and right after a therapy session. One father recently commented that his usually withdrawn son was significantly more cheerful and animated for a couple of days after he participated in therapy. He said, "I don't know what you are doing, but he seems to feel great after he has been here and I want him to come enough times that this change in him lasts through the week."

While some sensory integration therapeutic activities can have somewhat immediate effects on areas like attention, mood, language production, posture, and organizational skills, the most likely thing that a parent will notice is that their child enjoys and looks forward to the therapy sessions. Being in a situation where they are understood and supported, as well as helped to be successful, is often an empowering experience for children with sensory integration dysfunction.

The best way to determine that therapy is truly helping is to establish specific goals around the functional skills that are important for the child and family. For example, for a child with a sensory integrative problem that involves heightened sensitivity to touch, the functional goal might be the ability to tolerate having his hair or face washed without signs of discomfort. For another child with poor ability to coordinate actions of the two sides of the body, the functional goal might be pedaling a bicycle or mastering a swimming stroke. Because change is likely to occur gradually over time, documentation of the current functional issues through setting targeted goals is important so that the changes that are made can be measured. One mother told me, "I almost forgot how difficult our life used to be, now that things are so much easier. When I look back on the problems I listed six months ago, they seem like distant memories."

While acknowledging and documenting a child's initial problems is an important part of determining the effectiveness of therapy, this part of the process can sometimes have the effect of making parents (and even the child) more aware of the extent of the problem. Greater awareness of the degree of difficulty a child is having with everyday activities commonly occurs as the parent learns more about dysfunction in sensory integration. Therefore, a parent may feel that the problem is bigger than originally thought, before it starts to seem lessened.

Another pattern that occurs is for some children to demonstrate a degree of disorganization in behavior, emotional state or actions, before more efficient functions emerge. A child who is participating in therapy using a sensory integration approach may be experiencing sensations and challenges that are powerful, novel, and, at times, confusing. Since new ways of perceiving and interpreting information are occurring, some children may initially show some behaviors that are unexpected and possibly undesirable. For example, a child who has been very fearful may begin to feel less vulnerable and may suddenly start to take risks that seem dangerous. Or a child who craves movement activities during a therapy session may become highly active and talkative upon arriving home. Therapists and parents need to have close communication so that the therapist can be aware of the child's immediate and longer-term responses to therapeutic activities and can collaborate with the family concerning how to address the child's responses.

The effectiveness of therapy aimed at improving sensory integration function is hard to measure with test scores. Families commonly say things like, "Life is less stressful now," "School seems to be going better," "My child and I both feel less frustrated than before," and "Now my child has friends." These kinds of qualitative changes in daily life are the ultimate goal of this therapy approach.

March 6, 1976

Dear Phil:

Sure liked the tone of your last letter. Everything is going very nicely on schedule, Phil. Now I need to warn you that the euphoria expressed in your letter is also part of many people's schedule. In a few days, Phil, you will likely be down in the dumps again. When you get there, remember that you aren't going to stay that depressed. You will feel better again later. I hope that your mood swings begin to level off pretty soon, although I suppose you will have them to a certain extent all of your life. Most of us do.

Tunneling sounds great. Having to go through a tunnel without touching the sides is a perfect thing for you to do. The vestibular system relates us to space, so you are putting the vestibular input right to work.

Certainly, your therapy is what is helping you to be able to climb, and I am glad you have the urge. Climbing not only takes postural responses on the part of the body but also is highly dependent upon being able to relate oneself to space. We see this urge in a number of children when some of the basic aspects of vestibular mechanisms organization have been taken care of. Some boys and girls also get an urge to work puzzles, indicating they have achieved a better degree of that type of space perception.

Therapy certainly will help your coordination. Just how far it will take you we won't know until you are there.

Franklin always enjoys hearing your letters. He empathizes with you so much. When I read him the sentence about tennis being easy he said, "Phil's off his rocker. Tennis is *not* easy. I have watched them play it." The vestibular system is essential to interpreting what we see in relation to space, and ball games are one of the ultimate forms of that kind of space perception.

I had the best visit with your dad yesterday evening. It had been a long time since I had seen him. He mentioned that someday he would like to bring you out to California for a visit.

Love,
Jean

Therapy Continues

BY PHILIP R. ERWIN

BECAUSE MY SENSORY INTEGRATION problems weren't identified and acted upon until I was 14, we had a small window of opportunity to make up a lot of lost time. I now believe that I had spent so much effort up until 14 hiding—from my teachers, my peers, my fears—that I was in some ways frozen in time, out of sync with kids my own age. So, although I was beginning to process sensory information more effectively, I had to learn how to use new contexts and to assert myself in places formerly hostile to me and in ways previously alien to me.

Adolescence was upon me and performing the seemingly child-like activities of sensory integrative therapies was positioned to conflict with a biological need to begin—in my own perception—acting like a grown-up. With my nascent maturation came a new set of confusing reasons to be upset with the world. I see now in Jeanie's letters that it must have been hard for her to distinguish the signs of my disability (and my progress out of its shadow) from the forces created by my natural inclination to be a brooding youth.

Sensory integrative therapy ended, for the most part, at the end of ninth grade. I was done with the prep school after losing two more years of potential progress to ill-fitting, unresponsive academic institutions. In the coming fall I would start over again at Staples High School in the Westport, Connecticut, public school system. In the interim period something astounding was about to happen: *no summer school.* Instead I was going to go away to summer camp in Maine for a month. At 15 years of age, I had never been away from home. When I walked into my family's yard after a month away I was ready to start growing up. I had made the first real steps by discovering that new challenges and unfamiliar environments did not cause certain failure.

Staples High School was a different world. I was under the caring guidance of the special education department. I had Mrs. Locke, my guidance counselor, who would strong-arm me when I was pathetic, and strong-arm others if they didn't give me a chance. I had Mrs. Lane, my resource room teacher, who cajoled, comforted, guilt tripped, and pushed me to *try.* I had Mr. Bob May, my mentor. Bob got me into an internship in the local fire department—two half-days per week riding the trucks, using the gear, and exploring the trade. It would take hours for me to describe a fraction of what these people did for me. I can best sum it up by saying that they recognized that I was beginning to develop interests that had merit and had direct bearing on things that I might be doing if and when I got out of high school. They cleared the trails and greased the rails. After all of those years of being the square peg being pounded into round academic holes, I finally had people chopping the holes to fit me.

Late in tenth grade I got involved in an Explorer scout troop that practiced rescue and emergency medical skills. Through that group I found a volunteer ambulance corps in a nearby city where I could volunteer when I was 16. In late eleventh grade and for all of twelfth grade I was riding shifts two or three overnights per week (driving home at six in the morning to get ready for school) and for 24 hours on weekends. Just after I turned 17 I got my Emergency Medical Technician certificate. I also held down a variety of paying part-time jobs. I made two groups of friends with whom I kept in contact for many years, one in the emergency medical services world and one in the social world that developed in school. When I turned 18 (before I graduated from high school) I was crew chief on the ambulance in charge of patient care and trainees on my shift.

All of this was being done by someone who still couldn't square dance.

March 24, 1976

Dear Philip,

I wasn't particularly perturbed by you being a week late with your letter. I was thinking of you intermittently last week as I lectured for five days in a row in Newark, New Jersey. I'm still tired from it. It snowed a little while I was there. Lovely.

The occupational therapist who tested you was in attendance where I lectured. She asked about you and brought some material on both a school and a summer program for me to look at. She cares very much about how your learning problem is handled.

Now it's Saturday night and Franklin and I have been in Visalia a couple of days. In addition to visiting with your grandmother, we went up to the Valley so that I could speak at the school where your cousin J.D [Ayres] goes to school. The principal there asked me to see a few children who were having learning difficulties. My first reaction to the invitation was that there wouldn't be many severe logical irregularities in a small school in Lemon Cove where there are so few contaminants and the children have so many opportunities for vestibular stimulation when playing. But I was wrong—there were lots of them and most of them with vestibular problems. Wish there were someone to help them now.

I like the idea of your going to Staples High School and being in the extra help program. They are bound to understand you better there than they do at the school at which you are now going.

Those are good words you write about your coordination. That means that the vestibular sensory input is getting through to parts of the brain better. It's easier to improve coordination than the things that interfere with learning, but I would think that with the changes you show, learning would begin to be a little easier, too.

Love,
Jean

What Can I Do to Help?

BY ZOE MAILLOUX

THE MORE THAT A PARENT understands their child's challenges, the more helpful they can be. I often encourage parents to become "detectives" to help uncover the ways in which their child's sensory integration problem is making life difficult and to experiment with ways to help their child feel more comfortable and successful.

In addition to increased awareness, understanding, and support, families are also critical to the therapy process, itself. Seeking an evaluation and ensuring regular attendance in the recommended therapy program are the first steps. "Carry-over" of therapeutic principles, concepts and activities to the home, school, and community will provide the best possible outcome for any child.

Since we are used to lessons, exercises, and practice for learning new skills, parents often think they need a specific plan or program to perform at home in support of their child's sensory integration-based intervention. Fortunately, carry-over of the sensory integration approach can be quite natural and should actually be fun. As in the therapy session itself, a child will be more motivated and remain with an activity longer if it seems more like play than work. Daily routines of getting ready for school, preparing for mealtime, and winding down for bedtime can all be altered in ways that will "fit" a child's sensory integration needs. Many household tasks, such as cooking, doing laundry, and gardening, as well as leisure and play activities, provide natural opportunities for enriching sensory integration.

Parents often say that their child will not "cooperate" for them as well as they do for a teacher or therapist. This is to be expected, as children typically feel the most comfortable around their parents and thus can be their "true selves" at home. When parents begin to internalize the sensory integration concepts in a way that influences the way they think and interact with their child, the more likely the carry-over will feel acceptable to the child. In other words, parents need not try to be therapists. However, if they can be parents who use a sensory integration approach to parenting, they will help their children make the greatest gains possible.

April 8, 1976

Dear Phil:

Your letter brought me as close to tears as having your free period taken away from you did to you. One of the great disillusionments of my life—and probably of most people who grow up—is that this is not a just world. We are only endowed differently. Those of us who have problems not only have to cope with the problem, but we also have to cope with others' lack of understanding of the problem and their behavior toward us because of the problem. I see this over and over again, especially with those with neurological problems which are not recognized as neurological problems.

But was Mr. King really punishing you? Could he have been trying to put you in a situation that would make for better math grades? When will educators learn that if the existing approach does not work, maybe they better try another?

Our only way to cope is to know within ourselves that we are coping with a disadvantage that others do not have. If our actions meet with our own approval, then that is enough acceptance—and the most important acceptance.

This next section is for your mother, but you are welcome to read it, too. At Lemon Cove I spoke to teachers, a couple of school psychologists, and a principal. Parents were invited, but I think the only ones who came were Richard and Carmen [Ayres] and my own mother. I made the lecture as simple as possible and Richard said he could understand it. The teachers had watched me test about a dozen children and saw how much trouble they had with motor planning and postural reactions. That helped them to understand why these children were having learning and behavior problems. They are going to be looking at those hostile children with a very different perspective from now on, I think. I was very pleased that Richard asked me to do what I did and pleased that I could do something for him.

I surely look forward to your being in public school next year.

Love,
Jean

The Save

BY PHILIP R. ERWIN

MY JOB AS A PARAMEDIC for the City of New York's munici-pal emergency medical service created countless opportunities for personal challenge. My routine station assignments—the result of a competitive seniority-based bid system—allowed me to select different neighborhoods and different sub-cultures of the vast city in which to serve. I was able to move from the Bowery and the Lower East Side of Manhattan (freaks, bums, junkies, and plain folks getting by) to Coney Island, Brooklyn (heart attacks, geriatrics, complex medical calls, and plain folks getting by) to East New York/Brownsville, Brooklyn (desperate poverty, shootings, stabbings, O.D.s, violence, mayhem, and plain folks getting by) to the South East Bronx (all of the above). Staying at each station a few years enabled me to round out my skills and to see everything possible in the human con-dition many times.

One really fun assignment was an overtime gig available to a few of us in the field: The Dignitary Protection Unit. A joint task force composed of city cops, Secret Service protection teams, and paramedics, "Special One" was activated whenever high profile political persons were in town for speeches at ses-sions of the United Nations. Driving in the motorcades and staying in the best hotels with the Secret Service guys was a gas. When the protectee moved about town, we traveled with the motorcade with a Secret Service agent riding shotgun. Moving around Manhattan in a line of tightly spaced counter-attack vehicles, police cars, motorcycles, and limousines was challenging and fun. Staying at the Waldorf Astoria, one floor below the president of Egypt or the President of the United States, meant hanging out and eating room service with off duty federal bodyguards with their guards down and their briefcases and machine guns up on the windowsills. Of course, the underlying reason we were all there was pretty grim. During training for the team, we paramedics were disabused of any heroic notions.

"If something happens, duck," the federal agents confided, "Everyone standing when the shooting starts is going down. You're there for the survivors. Before you can help, we'll be long gone with the principal."

One of the less glamorous—and less fun—assignments on Special One was to have to spend the night in the MERV (The Mobile Emergency Room Vehicle). A large converted bus, the MERV was a mobile intensive care unit and operating room used in disasters. It was parked on a side street across from the hotel where the dignitary was staying. During one session of the U.N., which presidents from many nations were to attend, I was assigned to spend a night waiting in the bus with a guy whom I had gone through paramedic training with a few years before. Wally and I had not been particularly good friends during training, but we were certainly cordial and mutually interested due to our common background. We were also interested in hearing how the first years of our medic experiences had gone for one another, so we spent most of the uneventful night telling war stories.

Unlike units that are servicing the needs of the citizens on the 911 system, Special One was on the special operations frequency—we were not accountable to anyone's needs except those that might arise in a moment of crisis at the Waldorf. This meant we could catch some sleep on a stretcher while we waited through a quiet night earning overtime pay. At some point during the evening we were cleared—one at a time—to walk over to the hotel's ballroom and fill a tray up with dignitary food and go back to the MERV and eat. Sometime after 2:00 a.m., when it seemed unlikely that any Special Operations Division supervisors would be dropping in for a visit, we each chose a stretcher to lay down on and sack out.

The early morning pre-rush hour was well under way when I woke up. Horns and voices moved past the giant ambulance in a muted dissonance that meant that another workday for most people had begun. All I had to do was make it until 9:00 a.m. for my relief from the day tour and I could hop the F train home and finish my weekend. Wally mentioned that he was going to get a coffee and asked if I wanted anything. I told him, no, that I would hang with the truck until he got back and then go over to the hotel and wash up. I laid back on the stretcher and closed my eyes, drifting off again.

I was jolted awake when Wally slammed through the door and yelled that there was a woman passed out on Madison Avenue about 100 feet away. I remember kind of groaning at the idea of dealing with a drunk or a seizure before I had my morning coffee and grabbing the airway bag and portable radio and walking out with my partner to deal with it. From about 50 feet away I could see that the woman was well dressed and that a small, panicked crowd had gathered and was frantically waving and yelling to us. We jogged up and I saw that she was blue.

No pulse. No respirations. A cardiac arrest. We were unable to transport the woman off the sidewalk—the MERV is a stationary facility. I asked Wally to run back and get the drug box and EKG/defibrillator. I radioed operations and requested they put a call over to the Manhattan dispatcher for a medic unit to respond to our location. While Wally was gone, I got out the bag valve mask and gave her a few deep ventilations. I opened her shirt and performed a few rib-cracking chest compressions. I pulled out the laryngoscope—a long, stainless steel blade on the end of a cylinder with batteries in it. The scope is used by inserting the blade far down the throat of a patient and opening the airway. There is a light on the tip of the blade, powered by the batteries in the handle. One looks down the throat, between the vocal chords, and into the airway. While watching the cords, I inserted a foot-long hollow plastic tube between them and into her bronchial tubes before they bifurcate into left and right branches on their way to right and left lung. On the end of the tube is a balloon that I inflated to seal the tube into place and prevent "blowby" when I attached the bag valve mask and inflated her lungs. The crowd now numbered in the dozens.

Wally ran back with the rest of our gear. A foot patrol cop walked up and asked if he could help. We had him pump the woman's chest. We got the EKG machine hooked up to the three leads and pads that go on the chest and saw the chaotic rhythm of ventricular fibrillation—meaning the woman's heart had stopped and was merely jiggling in her chest, no rhythm, no pumping of oxygen-rich blood to her dying tissues. Wally charged the paddles to 200 watts and zapped her. Her body jumped; her heart did not. We buzzed her again at 300 watts this time. Her heart rhythm remained chaotic and non-productive. I opened the drug box—with one hand I ventilated the patient and with other I cracked open an epinephrine syringe (our drugs came in easy-to-assemble pre-packs that required screwing a clear glass cylinder full of drug into a plastic barrel with a needle on the end). I squirted 10 cc.s of 1:10,000 solution of epinephrine into the endotracheal tube and pumped in oxygen. Certain medications go well into the respiratory tract. Epinephrine works especially well until the IV is established and Wally was on that job quick.

With an IV established, I handed Wally two amps (88 milliequivilents) of sodium bicarbonate that he injected. We gave bicarb because the woman was probably acidotic from her lack of perfusion and gas exchange. We were buffering her system's out-of-whack pH to make it more sympathetic to our other treatments. I injected another milligram of epinephrine into her IV. We zapped her again at full power, 400 watts. Nothing. And still no back-up ambulance. Just us, the dying woman, and a crowd now nearing 40 horrified witnesses to this early morning drama. I suggested that we administer Bretyllium, a potent heart calming medication. Wally gave her a 5 milligram per kilogram of body weight injection. We shocked her again and got a very coarse rhythm.

"Got a pulse!" yelled Wally. The crowd sighed collectively and began to murmur.

I broke out the Lidocaine and gave the patient a 75-milligram injection and began preparing a 3-milligram per minute IV drip to add to her existing IV. Lidocaine (a Novocain derivative) is a powerful anti-dysrhythmia drug that is used to prevent the formerly jiggling heart, now beating in a regular rhythm, from degrading again into irritable confusion. We could hear sirens in the distance. The woman's heart rate began to drop. Her pulse was slowing. Wally asked for atropine. I handed him a syringe and he gave her half a milligram IV push. Atropine acts on the vagus and inhibits the nerve that slows the heart rate down in normal circumstances. Her heart rate picked up and we were able to detect spontaneous respirations and a blood pressure. When the Bellevue Hospital-based medic unit pulled up we had a live—albeit very sick—woman to transfer to their care. We explained what we had done and Sue and Claudia (two other former classmates who happened to be on regular duty that morning) took over patient care. Within two minutes they were off at high velocity with a post cardiac arrest.

Wally and I stood there in silence and looked around us. The crowd—packed around us just seconds before—had wandered off to whatever their day had in store for them. We stood in a pile of wrappers and syringes, bloody gauze and body fluids. We cleaned up and walked back to the MERV and waited for the day-tour shift to relieve us. It was difficult to know what to do next. That emergency on the street wasn't supposed to *happen*. We had just been minding our own business, getting some fine overtime, and *boom*, good-bye morning.

It turns out that more had been happening that morning than our little life-and-death act on the sidewalk on Madison Avenue. The Secret Service had videotaped the unfolding events from the roof of the Waldorf: real events in real time. The woman was someone of both importance and integrity from Greenwich, Connecticut. As a result, Wally and I got invited to the Secret Service Ball, a large affair at the Waldorf held at the end of the U.N. sessions, where we were honored for saving the woman's life. The woman thanked us later and resumed her life's path of triumphs and disappointments.

The cardiac arrest that we resuscitated that day was like only 24 others out of hundreds that I did in my time in New York in that this rare patient got her care fast and it worked. So many others, always worked on in full public view in their living rooms with their loved ones watching, or in restaurants, or on subways, or on sidewalks like this, didn't work. Too sick, too little, too late. But I tried and I got used to doing what I had to do, under enormous stress, with inconceivably important consequences, in a venue that held critics, troublemakers, pseudo-experts, and caring loved ones.

That act of public theater was something that paramedics craved. The bigger the risk, the hairier the call, the more chaotic and out of control the situation, the better. The paramedic trade is part adrenaline addiction and part human duty. The common factor was the potential to control the uncontrollable and reject biological entropy. Death was the enemy and we rode in opposition to it on the street

A. JEAN AYRES
TORRANCE, CA

April 24, 1976

Dear Phil:

It is a relief, isn't it, to be able to pinpoint some of your problems. Surely hope those vitamins and a low sugar diet will help you feel better. Wish we could solve more problems with pills. Easy and quick. Not much else in life is, is it?

Phil, you aren't going downhill in math; the rest of the class is going uphill. You are probably standing just about still. Since you never got the fundamentals of math down pat, you naturally can't get any of the more complicated processes that are dependent upon fundamentals. Sure wish you could find some teacher that would teach you step by step in a manner in which you could learn and have success.

I'll be glad when you are out of that school and are getting some special help from either the public school or Coleytown Center. Special help teachers are bound to be oriented in learning disabilities and understand your situation.

The last two days I have been listening to a physician from Buenos Aires who, like me, has found that a disorder in the vestibular system is often at the root of learning disabilities. If I had discovered his work—all in a foreign language—a decade ago it would have helped me considerably. Instead, it wasn't until I found out the importance of the vestibular system to learning that someone else interested in that system told me about an article in English published in Mexico. That article led to a number of things, including our inviting him to lecture in this area when he came to California. It is interesting that they have the same kinds of problems in Argentina that we have here—at least learning problems. This physician says that Argentina does not have a drug problem or a lot of the social problems the U.S. has. He attributes the difference in the drug problem to the fact that countries selling illegal drugs to the U.S. do so to get U.S. dollars, whereas the Argentina peso is not sought after. If I read the paper correctly Argentina has some problems in the political arena that the US at least has less of.

Shall we put the letter-writing exchange on a monthly basis now? You are past the stage where I feel I need to guide you in what you do and to encourage you to get to the point in which you can see that it is helping you in some way. Since you see that it is at least helping your coordination you will be motivated to continue, I hope. I like receiving your letters and I like writing you, but I don't think you should feel obligated to write every two weeks. Your visual space perception is a lot better, too. Your printing in this last letter was beautiful. Some of this improvement is bound to filter into the academic area, but you won't know it as long as everything is over your head all of the time.

I enjoyed your mother's letter.

Love,
Jean

Where Does Therapy Stop
and Life Begin?

BY ZOE MAILLOUX

As DIFFICULT AS IT CAN BE to find help for a child with sensory integration dysfunction, navigating the course of therapy, including knowing when to end intervention programs, can be even more confounding. Almost all children who have sensory integration problems are helped in some way when their problems are recognized and therapy is initiated. For some families, the changes may only be moderate, while for others intervention will bring dramatic improvement that alters the outlook for their child's future in significant ways. Whether gains are subtle or fantastic, the possibility that continued progress can only occur through continued intervention often hovers over families who see programs changing or coming to an end.

Unfortunately, the frequency, duration, and quality of almost all health- and educationally-related programs are too often determined by funding that is rarely adequate. This is a large socio-politico-economic issue that is beyond the scope of this discussion. For the moment, let's assume a situation where the funding for services is not an issue in determining the course of a child's therapy program. This is Michael's story.

We met Michael at the beginning of the book. His mother's message expressing her concerns about him reflected her confusion about his problems and her fears for his future. When Michael was tested at age 5, he displayed a pattern of sensory integration dysfunction that Dr. Ayres had identified early in her research. He had significant problems in sensory processing that involved the vestibular sensory system—a disorder that would be rarely identified if not evaluated by a professional with advanced training in sensory integration theory and practice. Dr. Ayres was particularly interested in children who had problems similar to those that Michael demonstrated during his evaluation, because they struggled so much in school and in many daily activities, yet were so poorly understood. Children with this type of sensory integration disorder are often bright and quite capable in many ways. Dr. Ayres worried that they would "fall between the cracks" and not receive the understanding or assistance they need. One of the things that struck Dr. Ayres about children like Michael was that they were typically very motivated to participate in therapy and often showed very good gains following intervention programs. So it was for Michael.

Following his evaluation, a parent conference was held to go over the results of the tests. In spite of the natural worry any mother might have upon hearing that her child had a problem, Michael's mother felt mostly relief at now having a name for the struggles she had witnessed in her child. Michael started receiving therapy right away, and like many other children who demonstrated a similar profile, he loved coming to his therapy sessions. Michael could not seem to get enough of the sensory-rich activities that were introduced during his intervention program. His parents were pleased that not only did Michael's mood and attitude seem brighter, but gradually his performance at school became less labored as well. His father said, "I don't know exactly what you are doing with him in therapy, but whatever it is, it is working. I have never seen him so happy and organized."

Michael's mother wanted to learn as much as she could so that she could help him at home. She understood that his young nervous system was still developing and she wanted to provide as much support as possible during his developing years. She and her husband soon found themselves thinking about functions of the brain in everyday ways. For example, on a camping trip, they found that they had divided up chores and had given Michael all the jobs that involved lifting, pushing, and pulling the gear and equipment. They realized that they had begun to inherently sense the kinds of tasks that Michael needed throughout his day to stay focused and productive. Michael's father built some swings and climbing equipment at home that were similar to the things used in his therapy sessions. Michael's siblings enjoyed these pieces of play equipment, as well. Michael, himself, became quite intrigued with understanding how his brain and nervous system worked. He even did his science project on the sensory systems, including the little-known vestibular sense.

After about a year of weekly therapy, Michael had made many gains. He now had access to many sensory activities at home and school and had developed a set of strategies to use to help him feel "put together." Michael's therapist noticed that he no longer seemed as driven to participate in therapy, although he was still cooperative. He had achieved most of the goals that had been established and the therapist had some trouble trying to identify new goals that really needed to be addressed. The therapist met with Michael's parents to talk about a plan for transitioning out of ongoing intervention.

Michael's mother expressed anxiety about "losing" help for Michael. Although she agreed that he had made good progress, she worried that he would regress without therapy. The thought of being left on her own to figure out what Michael needed was overwhelming. "What about when he goes to middle school and high school?" "Do you think he will have trouble in college?" "Will he have any trouble driving?"

Michael's therapist did not have the answers to these questions, but she knew that his family had immersed themselves in understanding his difficulties and had been dedicated to finding help and solutions to his problems. She said, "Michael may always have some challenges that are related to the sensory integration problems we identified a year ago. But now all of you are so well equipped to understand what is going on and what to do about it. You can always come back for help, if you ever need it."

Michael's mother felt relieved to know that the door was not being closed. She did call the therapist, somewhat frequently at first, and less as time passed. Michael asked about coming back to therapy occasionally, and did so a few times over the next year. The following summer, when his mother asked if he wanted to visit the therapy center, he said, "No, I don't think I need to go there anymore."

When parents do not face so many hurdles in finding the right help for their children initially and when they know that their safety nets will not be cut away based on arbitrary decisions, they will be likely to be most comfortable with the transitions that are part of any intervention program. Understanding and help for children like Michael are far more accessible than they were during the time that Dr. Ayres first developed her ideas. She might be surprised to see how many of her concepts are now a common part of many programs. Still, we have a long way to go.

A. JEAN AYRES
TORRANCE, CA

October 5, 1976

Dear Phil:

Yes, I felt quite sad as I left Boston Sunday to return to L.A. after I had been imagining for months leaving and down to Connecticut and seeing all the Erwins. One doesn't always get what one would like from life. So I am back in Torrance and making arrangements to join with others to purchase a lot on which we will build a commercial building, part of which I will be leasing for the tremendous rent of $8000 a year. Takes courage—as well as money.

It certainly was good to hear from you, Phil, but please do not feel the need to apologize for not writing. Write when you feel like it.

What I liked most about your letter was your message that everything is going so well. Apparently you are in a school that recognizes your learning disability and handles it appropriately. I think I would raise a stink about being put in advanced basketball. That will just cause you pain.

Phil, what happens to you when you take a test happens to a lot of people. As far as I can tell, not being able to do one's best on an exam is most apt to be related to anxiety. You have been placed in overly demanding positions (academically) so often that you probably become very anxious at exam time and that anxiety reduces your ability to think of what you already know. Here are two things you could do about it. Talk to your mom about how you feel about the test before you go to school. Try not to repress any feelings of anxiety—talk about them. That will help to relieve them, not make them worse. The best thing I know to do to change the neural state that we experience as anxiety is transcendental meditation. Get [your brother] Don to tell you about it sometime when he is home. Someday you will want to see what that procedure can do for you. It does more to set my brain straight when I am upset than anything else. I don't think I could get through two days of lecturing without it. I use it to take the place of sleep, sometimes. When I travel, sometimes I get only 3 hours of sleep because I cannot sleep. Using the meditation technique (which is, I think, really learning to activate the alpha waves of the brain) helps make up for the lack of sleep. This technique might also change the ongoing neuronal activity to make it easier for you to concentrate and learn in the first place.

Using the sense of touch to help you learn is certainly worth trying. Using several sensory systems at a time may help to make up for what you are not able to get through your eyes. Impulses from the muscles and joints are probably helpful, too. I'm glad you are taking typing. It is such a good thing to be able to do. Alas, I am never going to master it. I just don't have the circuitry for it.

Sure glad you like firefighting. Mighty essential people, firemen are.

Love,
Jean

Changes

BY PHILIP R. ERWIN

RECENTLY I'VE BEEN LOOKING BACK on many of my life experiences using a lens honed with the grit that comes from living with sensory integration problems and learning disabilities. It is my view that any successes that I have enjoyed can be attributed directly to three external factors: My parent's tireless advocacy on my behalf, my aunt's clinical intervention towards righting my sensory integration shortfalls, and my high school teachers' and counselors' willingness to cut trails into new, nontraditional educational territories for me.

While I understand how the first and the last factors worked—my parents tenaciously seeking and re-directing potential solutions to my problems and my teachers forging frameworks of potential success for me—I return periodically to a question about what my Aunt Jeanie did. I mean that I understand (remember quite acutely, actually) the immediate effects her therapies had *on* me. I know what sensory integrative therapy did *for* me. It changed me from a worn-down kid avoiding new experiences into a self-actualizing person capable of seeking successes physically, emotionally, and intellectually. My question is this: what did sensory integration therapy do *to* me?

Before sensory integration therapy I had dyscalculia. After

therapy—and to this day—I remain significantly arithmetically challenged. Prior to therapy I was shy, a benign social recluse. I remain shy and self-contained nearly 30 years later. Although I manage my life now in a fairly organized manner, the tipping point between order and chaos remains palpable and immediate to me in all of my daily choices. That tipping point was a dominant force in my very confused universe before I underwent sensory integration therapy. Looking back to my pre-therapy days, when I neither could or would play in the physical athletic world, it seems strange that the post-therapy me has lived, worked, and played successfully, consistently, and with joy in this previously hostile realm. So if sensory integration therapy didn't "cure" me of the so called disabilities that I continue to present as core attributes of who I have always been, what did Jeanie do to me that allowed me to experience such a remarkable transformation?

In my first career as an emergency paramedic, the skill sets that I utilized every day were premised on the ability to memorize and accurately recall dozens of complex, multi-step, multi-option patient treatment algorithms. The administration of injectable medications, IV solutions, and therapeutic electrical shocks are controlled by mathematical calculations that factor dosages in grams, milligrams, micrograms, and millivolts given a patient's weight in kilograms. The training program that I went to courtesy of the New York City emergency medical system was brutally competitive. Attrition of the starting class to the final 50 or 60 percent that reached graduation was controlled by daily quizzes and weekly exams, all of which demanded memorization, organization, and calculation.

When I moved on from my paramedic career to get my university degree, I had accrued many victories as an adult—professional success, strong friendships and relationships, economic solvency—but still lived in an academic vacuum created by a horrific high school grade point average and an anemic performance on the SAT that reflected that I often randomly filled the dots in on computer answer cards (even on this "important" test) out of boredom and apathy. I had no academic cachet. I was strictly vocational.

I started taking college classes part time as a non-admitted undergraduate. Since I was not admitted, I didn't have to prove I could function. I merely paid and attended. After two quarters of this I was able to apply for admission based on my performance up to that point. I quickly worked my way into receiving an honors scholarship. I got brave and tried to take a pre-college algebra course (the same principles that I had been locked up in summer school to learn over and over again as a kid). I barely got out alive. So, again, some things had not changed.

As my date with commencement neared and I was making my post-university plans, I reached a crossroads. I had been able to convince a few graduate programs to offer me admission even though my application essays hardly reflected serious intentions. I had wrung dry my major in Philosophy by the end of my four years. In asking for admission to graduate programs I was essentially telling the administrators that I wanted to sign on to one dogma or another. I had a hard time convincing myself of the value of doing that and probably did no better at convincing them.

The other option that presented itself was to study wooden boat and yacht restoration and construction as an apprentice. What was involved was descriptive geometry, mathematics, measuring, machines, wood sciences, physical labor, and historic craft concepts all of which resulted in physical manifestations of newly tried ideas. After three years of study, I was hired as a vocational instructor to teach these same skills to 36 apprentices over the next three years. I excelled as an instructor.

After three years I left teaching to work as a shipwright in the commercial world, starting my own company, bidding jobs, and assuming sole responsibility for the economic health of both my business and my household. Again, why did I find success in territories that would have defeated the pre-therapy me? My vocational compass sets courses into life scenarios that would have hostile potential for a person such as I might have become without sensory integration therapy.

Looking back, I remember the feeling of calm that came over me as I went through the therapy regimen so long ago. Before I started scooter boarding, I felt like I was trapped in an exoskeleton. I was all corners and edges. I moved in limited, uncomfortable patterns. When my bony carapace and I bumped into unexpected objects, my hardness made compromise impossible. I had to back up and yield. I had to constantly pick routes through life that wouldn't trap my bones and me in tight corners or dead ends out of which I would be unable to extricate myself. But after scooter boarding for a while my hard, exterior shells fell away. I became suppler. When I met an obstacle I was often able to move delicately around it, perhaps squeeze by it, or mold myself into a shape or configuration more in harmony with it. After months of therapy, I had shed and regrown my shell many times but less and less of it grew back after each shedding.

What Jeanie and sensory integration therapy did *to* me was to re-wire me. While I experienced little improvement in my mathematical abilities, I was able to construct collateral strategies that circumvented my shortcomings. My brain became more organized, less threatened by all of the things that the world was asking of it. *I could pay attention.* With these fundamental changes, coupled with the support from my family and the validation of my teachers, I was able to utilize a host of coping skills that had been previously been looked down upon or discouraged (such as counting on my fingers, or saying, "So what if I don't know my times tables, I'll solve it some other way").

Although I remain shy (a personal trait that my parents feel I inherited from them), therapy—this re-wiring—interrupted the devastating circuit that had dominated my life before: the attempts, the failures, and the public humiliations (or perceptions of such). Developing my underdeveloped sensory integration system allowed me to start categorizing and organizing all of the input from the physical world into terrains that I could finally recognize, map, and navigate. With the de-fanging of novel experiences I have been able to try whatever pleases or interests me—and still be the shy me that I am in acceptable proportions. With the world more orderly, my quiver of coping skills more full—no longer lurching around teetering piles of potential failure—I have been able to divert my dreams around comparatively simple learning disabled-based deadends.

December 8, 1976

Dear Phil,

You can type slow and accurately or fast and sloppily; I can type fast and sloppily or slow and still sloppily. Sure glad you can type. It would be such a help to me to be able to type well, but I just don't have the circuitry for learning well.

I am mighty glad that you are finally in a school situation that understands you and provides you with appropriate instructional material and help. I share your good feeling.

Those are good words about firefighting, too. Does it seem as though it is either overly exciting or boring? Fires aren't consistent. There was a time when firefighters refurbished toys during the non-busy time. What do they do now? I suppose you have things to learn so that you don't have the time on your hands that the regular firemen have.

I feel sad with you about not having a consistent friend. Thank goodness you have a close family to help make up for it. Now that some of the school pressure is off you and you are feeling better about yourself it may become easier for you to make friends. Remember that there are a lot of other people with the same or similar problems to yours and those people may be having trouble making friends, too. One of the factors that makes for successful friendship among people with problems is being accepting of the other person even with his problems. A lot of allowances need to be made on both sides. There are no doubt a lot of people who would feel good about having you accept them just the way they are.

I agree with your art teacher. You always have been good at design, even when you were small.

My car has gone 112,000 miles, and it is beginning to show it. I had to be towed off the freeway today. Insulation in the wires caught on fire. Sure was great to be able to call my husband to come get me when I finally got to a garage.

Tell your mom thanks for the letter.

Hope a good year is ahead of you, Phil.

Love,
Jean

Stone Soup

BY PHILIP R. ERWIN

THE POEM OF LIFE is broken into verse and stanza by moments both significant and small as we write it, or better, as it is written for us. We are not the poets. We are the poem. The poets are time, experience, and the benevolence of others.

The large breaks in our poems, the white spaces on the page that create pause and re-direction, indicate that one's life trajectory has been shifted dramatically for better or to our detriment. These are remembered not like we remember where we were when President Kennedy was assassinated. Instead we recall the hour that we perceived ourselves as adults in our relationships for the first time. Perhaps the birth or death of a loved one caused us to feel joy or regret to a sufficient degree that we became someone new. It may have been a significant personal success or failure that affected our gravity and spun us off in new directions.

For me my poem changed from a simple, innocent, Dr. Seuss-like rhyme to something dark and complex when I perceived that I was not a successful kid. It changed again into a song of revelation and hope when I awoke from the darkness of my failure and was given a new start through therapy that integrated my senses. My trajectory shifted at distinct points, marking the following paradigm shifts in my reality:

- From happy kid to my "child feeling hopeless" period.
- Then into my child bursting into new lights of hope and confidence.
- Then again when my young man became unafraid to confront and embrace a life of contrasts and challenges, breaking the bonds of youthful uncertainty.
- And then onward to waypoints where I visited life and death in intimate and undisguised circumstances.
- From depleted human wreckage, I experienced physical and spiritual regeneration as I was transformed into an athletic adventurer.
- The death of my first career and my rebirth into a life of the mind was the prequel to my shift into a life of craft and the need to prove that the life of the philosopher-craftsperson was as possible as it was good.

1988 brought me to a significant turning point when I regained my physical and emotional health following the degenerative rigors of my life as a New York City paramedic. I moved from the city to the suburbs. I moved up the professional ladder as I participated in a high performance emergency medical system as a caregiver and educator. I was geographically close to my parents, which allowed me to re-connect to them in ways that have created lasting, loving friendships with them both.

In 1988, two old friends and I traveled to Los Angeles to visit a fourth good friend who was living and working there. I took the opportunity to call Jeanie and arrange to have lunch with her in Torrance at her home on a hill overlooking the Pacific Ocean.

My pals and I were only going to be in Los Angeles for 48 hours. They assumed (as many young twenty-something's would) that my visit was one of familial obligation rather than a deeply important personal journey that I urgently felt the need to undertake.

I hadn't seen Jeanie since I had gone through, completed, and benefited from the sensory integrative therapies she had conducted by "remote control" through my mom some years before. She was now sick with cancer.

I had to negotiate with the guys—they wishing me to do a drive-by visit of sorts, and I wishing I could spend more time than we had. They would drop me off at eleven and pick me up at one. I had two hours.

I was nervous when they dropped me off. I suppose my nervousness came from my natural shyness—but even more, I think it came from the wave of emotions that I felt as I walked up to the door. "Here I am," I felt like screaming. "It worked! You saved my life!"

Jeanie was very small and delicate—even smaller than my mom, her sister. I remember clearly the warmth of her hug and the delicate fragility of her frame. I felt a home feeling, an indelible family feeling. Perhaps a genetic memory of our connection. I was unafraid and comforted to be with her.

The house was dark and cool. It was very quiet. Franklin, Jeanie's husband, was out and it would just be my aunt and myself for lunch.

Jeanie had set the table by the sliding doors with simple brown bowls. She said that she hoped that I would like lunch, that it might not be to my liking. She said, "I've made stone soup."

Stone soup? Jeanie was seeking help from many sources for her illness. Her diet was among the changes that she had made towards that effort. The soup she offered that day was hot and good. It was a rough soup, simply flavored.

We ate quietly—a family trait I guess. It was quiet, but not uncomfortable. We merely ate in one another's company and enjoyed the peace and simplicity of that good activity. We talked about what I was doing and she told me how important my work was.

My work…important? I explained that my work was a by-product of her work—on me. I told her that she had saved my life and I thanked her. I told her how I became alive following her therapies. I told her how I felt that my life was composed of infinite possibilities rather than obstacles presenting dubious opportunities for success.

My friends pulled up in front of the house—two hours had passed! I wasn't ready to go. I needed to stay just a little longer. I needed to recite my life poem for my aunt—my poet—and I wasn't quite done. I told the guys to go to the beach or get some lunch, but to give me more time.

Jeanie and I sat on the sofa for a while and we talked about her work and where it was going. She told grownup things about her struggle to overcome an establishment that rejected her ideas and placed roadblocks to her progress. We talked about our family.

The boys pulled up again. Another hour had passed in but moments and I had to go this time.

Jeanie walked me to the door and thanked me for taking the time to see her. She thanked *me*. My God! As I hugged her good-bye, I tried to pass my love and gratitude from my body to hers. Goodbye quietly. I turned and walked to the guys in the car—young guys pumped up for wild times in L.A.

I waved as we drove off, feeling grateful for the afternoon over stone soup. Happily innocent of the truth that I had seized my last and only chance to thank my aunt for saving my life— for giving me a life. I had sung my poem well.

February 25, 1983

Dear Philip,

Franklin and I recently had a real treat: your mother visited us en route to Crestline, then Visalia. Her tales of some of your experiences astound me. Your job requires more emotional stamina than most of us have. I certainly admire your ability to handle the necessary and difficult job.

When I learned some months ago that you were going to petition for a waiver from passing the math of the paramedics exam and that you had a letter from an educator to attach to the waiver request, I was worried. I doubt very much that the examining board would be as sympathetic as the special educator. When your mother recently said the letter had been stolen from your car before you could present it, I was relieved.

Unfortunately, I don't have any better approach to suggest. I can pass on to you what I would do, but what I would do is not necessarily the best thing for you to do. I would keep taking the test, and after each taking I would quickly write down each math problem I could remember—then get the correct answer from somebody and try to memorize the answer. Maybe in time I would memorize enough answers to pass the test. I would also inquire as to whether comparable tests were available for study and try to memorize the math questions on them.

I sure hope you keep trying and someday make it.

Love,
Jean

A Look Back in Wonder

BY PHILIP R. ERWIN

I DIDN'T WANT TO LEAVE my room when I was a kid. I didn't want to compete with other kids. I didn't want to fail again in front of anyone. I got homesick—to the point of physical illness—when I was away from home. Other households seemed hostile and loud. Home was my safe zone.

Many years later—long after I had ceased rolling around on my scooter board—my career as a paramedic had taken me from New York City to Stamford, Connecticut, to Monterey and Big Sur, California, and finally to Klamath Falls, Oregon. I had enjoyed successes and suffered failures in each emergency medical system. The successes were the result of having the ability to integrate sensory input in the worst possible circumstances and function at a high level of competence. My failures were the result of my tendency towards boredom, and making trouble in the face of it. Once a situation was routine—an irony in the "life and death business"—I felt compelled by forces deep in my spirit to make it somehow new.

New locations worked for a while. But the novelty of the new place wore off quickly and I became dulled and restless. In the end, however, I could no longer move and I couldn't bear the idea of merely working for the paycheck alone. Many moves had left me where I started each time. It was evident that at 31 years of age that it was time to "retire."

When I finally burned out, I was living in southern Oregon. I moved from Klamath Falls to the small town of Ashland on the other side of the Cascade Mountains. While I began my pursuit of a college degree there, I continued following my passion for outdoor sport. Still no fan of team anything, I had been biking, hiking, and paddling (canoe and kayak) passionately since my Connecticut days five years before. Ashland had it all. I hiked all over the West, paddled isolated mountain lakes and streams, and got very alone in magnificent places. And every day I went for bike rides in the mountains around my town.

My favorite daily ride was the Ashland Loop. Leaving the historic mining-era town via the stunning city park a few hundred yards from my house, I climbed nine miles up a fire road through pine forests and past roiling streams. Once I hit the plateau beneath Mount Ashland, I turned onto a loop fire road that ran out into the watershed and back to the other side of the canyon for about 15 miles. Then it was eight miles downhill and I was back home, ready to go to class.

One day I packed up some water and Power Bars and headed out on the loop. Early morning in the summer in the Siskiyou Mountains of southern Oregon—before the afternoon heat shuts everything down—is a blissful time and a place to be by one's self. The air is dry and cool and perfumed with pine and dry soil. I remember feeling strong.

The rides always went the same way. I rode the first two or three miles under protest. I would argue internally, "turn back… no, next rise, then decide." I always stopped at a flat spot with an overlook and drank water. When I resumed pedaling, my mind and my body went their separate ways. My legs and lungs operated without my input. Just pumping and ventilating. Miles passed and the elevation grew. My mind was free to wander. Sometimes I daydreamed or fantasized; other times I sorted out problems or raged.

This particular morning in the mountains I have no idea what I was thinking except that I was experiencing peace in my strength and bliss in my surroundings. At the apex of the ride, nine miles up and 15 miles out from the nearest road or settlement, I was jerked from my inner world by a sudden pain on my chest. I skidded to a stop and dropped the bike. I pulled my shirt off and a dead bee fell out. In the middle of my breastbone there was a small but growing angry red spot where I had been stung.

When I was a kid I was once stung by a yellow jacket. It was my second sting and I had suffered an allergic reaction. Visits to the allergist every Saturday left me with an untested and unverified resistance to stings and an emergency bee-sting kit in the refrigerator. I had no further entanglements with bees until this moment up on the trail—immunity and bee kit long since expired. Some of the most horrifying calls that I went on as a paramedic were anaphylactic shock patients, as they were difficult or plain impossible to manage. Many were in cardiac arrest by time I arrived, some permanently.

I picked my bike up and rolled over to the edge of the fire road and sat down with my legs over the edge of the drop-off. And I thought. I was around 24 miles from any kind of help. The onset of anaphylaxis takes a few minutes at best. Then your blood pressure drops below a point at which you can remain conscious in an upright position. Your body begins pumping out histamine and your upper airways begin to swell. Large, itchy welts develop on your skin. You suffocate while your cardiovascular system collapses. The cure is a combination of aggressive supportive therapy, such as endotracheal intubation and positive pressure ventilation, large amounts of IV fluids, IV epinephrine to constrict your blood vessels and reduce swelling in your airways, IV Benedryl to counteract the histamines being produced by your stricken body, and a very fast ride to an emergency room. I had none of this available in the Ashland Watershed that morning.

So, I waited. I sipped some water. I smelled the pines. I listened to the needles hush in the breeze. I watched a hawk soar. I waited to see if I was going to die by the side of the road. I must say that what I experienced during those minutes of not knowing is certainly a most human set of emotions. I mean, I was pretty sure I wasn't going to die; it had been so long since the last sting, I certainly would have known by *now* that I was actually at risk. But, then again, I really did not know. All that I knew that morning was that I was alone, beyond help, and stuck with whatever happened.

Two minutes, then ten passed, and all I had was a little, itchy red bump on my chest. The air was breezy and sweet. The hills stood, the trees swayed, a hawk soared overhead, and I was alive. It was the perfect moment! It was the moment that I had been hiding from in my bedroom as a kid. It was the experience that I had been seeking since I moved to New York to be a paramedic. I had been challenged by circumstances undetermined by human competition but instead constructed by an immediate participation in my environment.

As I pedaled back to town, I soared with the hawk. I giggled and whooped all the way down the last drop and skidded into my driveway. I tried to call some of my friends so that I could explain the few moments of purity that I had experienced up in the hills by myself. I had finally proven to my most persistent detractor that I was game—really game—and could face the consequences of my choices. My choices in life had been vindicated. I was and remain unafraid of change and challenge. The only thing that I fear now is the lack of opportunity to seek new chaos. My only dread is the lack of trees to fall out of and bees to sting me.

Glossary

❖

In her book *Sensory Integration and the Child,* A. Jean Ayres writes: "The purpose of words is communication...If you don't know the meaning of our words, you cannot understand our ideas." If your child is diagnosed with dysfunction in sensory integration, it will be to your benefit to expand your understanding of the concepts behind the words that therapists employing sensory integrative techniques will use. Here are the terms Zoe Mailloux and Jean Ayres introduce in *Love, Jean.*

ADAPTIVE RESPONSE: An appropriate action in which the individual responds successfully to some environmental demand. Adaptive responses require good sensory integration, and they also further the sensory integrative process.

AUTISM: A form of brain disorder affecting the child's ability to relate to people, things, and events.

BILATERAL INTEGRATION: A neurological process integrating sensations from both sides of the body.

BRAIN MODULATION: The brain's regulation of its own activity. Modulation involves facilitating some neural message to maximize a response, and inhibiting other messages to reduce irrelevant activity.

CEREBRAL HEMISPHERES: The two large sections of the brain that lie over and around the brain stem. The hemispheres continue the sensory processing that begins at lower levels and assist in producing voluntary motor responses and behavior.

DYSFUNCTION OF SENSORY INTEGRATION: An irregularity or disorder in the brain function that makes it difficult to integrate sensory input effectively. Sensory integrative dysfunction may be present in motor, learning, social/emotional, speech/language, or attention disorders.

DYSLEXIA: Severe difficulty in using or understanding language while listening, speaking, reading, writing, or spelling.

LEARNING DISABILITIES: A difficulty in learning to read, write, compute, or do schoolwork that cannot be attributed to impaired sight or hearing, or to mental retardation.

MOTOR PLANNING: The ability of the brain to conceive of, organize, and carry out a sequence of unfamiliar actions. Also known as praxis.

NERVOUS SYSTEM: The central nervous system, and especially the brain, is designed to organize countless bits of sensory information into a whole integral experience.

OCCUPATIONAL THERAPY: Occupational therapy is a health profession concerned with improving a person's occupational performance. In a pediatric setting, the occupational therapist deals with children whose occupations are usually players, preschoolers, or students. The occupational therapist evaluates a child's performance in relation to what is developmentally expected for that age group. If there is a discrepancy between developmental expectations and functional ability, the occupational therapist looks at a variety of perceptual and neuromuscular factors which influence function. Based on knowledge of neurology, kinesiology, development, medical diagnoses, and current research, the occupational therapist can identify the children who have the best potential for remediation through occupational therapy.

PHYSICAL THERAPY: Physical therapy is a health profession concerned with improving a person's physical ability. In a pediatric setting, the physical therapist evaluates a child's orthopedic structure and neuromuscular functions. A physical therapist can also receive special training to assess and remediate the disorders in sensory processing that influence learning and behavior.

PHYSICIAN: A licensed medical practitioner who diagnoses illnesses and prescribes and administers treatment for people suffering from injury or disease.

PLASTICITY: The ability of the brain to change or to be changed as a result of activity, especially as one responds to sensations.

POSTROTARY NYSTAGMUS: A series of automatic, back-and-forth eye movements. Different conditions produce this reflex. A common way of producing them is by an abrupt stop following a series of rotations of the body. The duration and regularity of postrotary nystagmus are some of the indicators of vestibular system efficiency.

PRONE: The horizontal body position with the face and stomach downward.

PSYCHIATRIST: A branch of medicine concerned with the diagnosis, treatment and prevention of mental illness. Psychiatrists can prescribe medicines, whereas clinical psychologists cannot.

PSYCHOLOGIST: A scientist trained in study of human behavior and the mind's function. The practice of psychology is defined as rendering or offering to render for a fee to individuals, groups, organizations or the public any psychological service involving the application of psychological principles, methods, and procedures of understanding, predicting, and influencing behavior, such as the principles pertaining to learning, perception, motivation, emotions, and interpersonal relationships; and the methods and procedures of interviewing, counseling, psychotherapy, behavior modification, and hypnosis; and of constructing, administering, and interpreting tests of mental abilities, aptitudes, interests, attitudes, personality characteristics, emotions, and motivations.

SPEECH AND LANGUAGE PATHOLOGIST: Speech-language pathologists assess, diagnose, treat, and help to prevent speech, language, cognitive, communication, voice, swallowing, fluency, and other related disorders. Speech-language pathologists work with people who cannot make speech sounds, or cannot make them clearly; those with speech rhythm and fluency problems, such as stuttering; people with voice quality problems, such as inappropriate pitch or harsh voice; those with problems understanding and producing language; those who wish to improve their communication skills by modifying an accent; and those with cognitive communication impairments, such as attention, memory, and problem solving disorders. They also work with people who have oral motor problems causing eating and swallowing difficulties. A speech-language pathologist can also receive special training to assess and remediate the disorders in sensory processing that influence learning and behavior.

SCOOTER BOARD: A scooter board consists of a piece of wood mounted on four wheels that can roll freely and spin in any direction. The board is big enough to support the middle part of the child's body, while his head, upper chest, and legs hang off the ends. It is usually covered by carpet or matting so that lying on it is comfortable.

SENSORY INTEGRATION: The organization of sensory input for use. The "use" may be a perception of the body or the world, or an adaptive response, or a learning process, or the development of some neural function. Through sensory integration, the many parts of the nervous system work together so that a person can interact with the environment effectively and experience appropriate satisfaction.

SENSORIMOTOR: Pertaining to the brain-behavior process of taking in sensory messages and reacting with a physical response.

SENSORY INPUT: The streams of electrical impulses flowing from the sense receptors in the body to the spinal chord and brain.

SENSORY INTEGRATION PRAXIS TESTS (SIPT): A series of tests published in 1989, designed to assess the status of sensory integration and praxis (motor planning) in children ages 4 through 8 years old.

VESTIBULAR NUCLEI: The groups of cells in the brain stem that process vestibular sensory input and send it on to other brain locations for organization of a response. These complex "business centers" also integrate vestibular input from other sensory channels.

VESTIBULAR SYSTEM: The sensory system that responds to the position of the head in relation to gravity and accelerated or decelerated movement; it integrates neck, eye, and body adjustments to movement.

VISUAL PERCEPTION: Pertaining to the interpretation of the sense of sight.

Index

About the Authors

A. JEAN AYRES, PhD, OTR. About 50 years ago, A. Jean Ayres, working as an occupational therapist with neurologically disabled children and adults, began to realize that the weak muscles and poorly coordinated hands and legs of these clients were not always their most severe handicaps. Some children could not put puzzles together, had trouble learning to dress themselves, and were unable to pay attention to any task longer than a few minutes. She focused her efforts on children with perceptual, learning, and behavior problems that could not be attributed to known causes. Her approach differed from that of other professionals in that she believed that the best answers would be found in a better understanding of how the brain processes sensations from not only the eyes and ears but other parts of the body as well. She is credited with founding the field of sensory integration

Dr. Ayres earned advanced degrees from the University of Southern California and undertook post-doctoral work at the Brain Research Institute at the University of California at Los Angeles. She was on the faculty of the University of Southern California for over 20 years. She is the author of *Sensory Integration and the Child, Sensory Integration and Learning Disorders*, and the Sensory Integration Praxis Tests. Every year, the American Occupational Therapy Association gives the A. Jean Ayres Award to occupational therapy clinicians, educators, and researchers who have demonstrated a sustained commitment to the application, development, or testing of theory in occupational therapy. A. Jean Ayres passed away in 1988.

PHILIP R. ERWIN. Mr. Erwin received his bachelor's degree in Philosophy from the University of Oregon, certificates in Advanced Emergency Medical Technician/Category 4 Paramedic, Advanced Cardiac Life Support, Pre-Hospital Trauma Life Support, and Pediatric

Advanced Life Support from the Einstein School of Medicine's Institute of Emergency Medicine, and a Third-year Advanced Restoration Fellowship from the International Yacht Restoration School. Prior to advancing his career as a writer and shipwright, he taught wooden boat restoration at the International Yacht Restoration School in Newport, Rhode Island, and served as a paramedic and emergency medical technician in New York, Connecticut, California, and Oregon.

ZOE MAILLOUX, MA, OTR, FAOTA. Ms. Mailloux is nationally and internationally recognized within the profession of occupational therapy in the area of sensory integration theory and practice. She is currently the Director of Administration at Pediatric Therapy Network, a non-profit children's therapy center serving over 1000 children and their families. With nearly 100 therapists, teachers and support staff, Pediatric Therapy Network provides therapeutic programs to 250 schools and community agencies, in addition to being the site of an intensive post-graduate training program for therapists offered through the University of Southern California. Ms. Mailloux has also participated in test development and clinical research related to sensory integrative dysfunction and autism. She was a research assistant to Dr. A. Jean Ayres from 1978 to 1984 and was involved in many clinical and research projects with Dr. Ayres. In addition, she has published numerous journal articles and textbook chapters on these topics. Ms. Mailloux was chairperson of the Sensory Integration Special Interest Section of the American Occupational Therapy Association from 1993 to 1996 and was named a fellow of this organization in 1993. She recently received an award of excellence from the Autism Research Foundation and was named the Wilma West Lecturer at the University of Southern California.

In Gratitude

❖

WE ARE INDEBTED to the staff of Pediatric Therapy Network for their review of this book for its technical accuracy. In addition to undertaking primary research on sensory integration in conjunction with the University of Southern California (from where A. Jean Ayres received all of her degrees and with which she was affiliated throughout her professional life), PTN's staff helps hundreds of children and provides in-school therapy for over 250 schools and agencies. Pediatric Therapy Network is a 501-C3 non-profit, meaning your donations may be tax deductible.

Pediatric Therapy Network
1815 213th St. #100
Torrance, CA 90501
213/328-0276
www.pediatrictherapynetwork.com

About Crestport Press

OUR MISSION

We at Crestport Press believe that the best way our books can affect change is for our authors to state their positions boldly, present their beliefs unvarnished to the world, and then let the power of the written word affect change from the outside in. Our books express our authors' deepest passions and their commitment to their values and beliefs.

WHAT YOU CAN DO

If this book has positively impacted your life, you can help the authors affect change by letting others know of their book's existence. Think about others of your acquaintance who are at a point in life where reading this book would have great meaning. Talk to them, phone them, or email them. Let them know that these authors have created a work that could expand their lives.

BULK PURCHASE DISCOUNTS

If you wish to receive a discount on orders of 10 or more copies of *Love, Jean* or any other Crestport Press product, contact us at:

Crestport Press
5021 Gregory Court
Santa Rosa, CA 95409
707-537-0580
www.cresport.com
info@crestport.com

Other A. Jean Ayres Works
Published by Crestport Press

www.crestport.com

A. Jean Ayres Lecture Series

Aspects of the Somatomotor Adaptive Response and Praxis
By A. Jean Ayres

In this lecture, delivered by A. Jean Ayres on June 26, 1981 in Cincinnati, OH, she proposes that "praxis does more than help us motor plan; it is a major element in the organization of non-reflexive, non-emotionally-based behavior, but it is not entirely unrelated to the latter." Her conclusions, gleaned from literature search, brain research, and observations of clients in her clinic "coalesced into a major insight: that praxis, or adaptive-response capacity, developed during sensory integrative procedures, generalizes to behavior beyond motor performance. It generalizes to more cognitive behavior, and possibly does so through enhancing a central programming mechanism for function of the brain."
(ISBN 0-9725089-2-8; 72 pages; $29.95)

Tools and Gifts for Therapist's and Parents

The Sensory Integration Booklet: Answers for Parents
By the Staff at the the Pediatric Therapy Network

This succinct booklet is a wonderful tool for therapists and parents who are embarking together on a child's journey towards sensory integration. Enhanced by photographs by Shay McAtee, one of A. Jean Ayres's first graduate students and a leading sensory integration theorist and clinician, you will have a handy guide to the basic principles and language with which you will want to be fluent. Available for bulk purchase through Crestport Press.
(ISBN 0-9725089-4-4; 16 pages $4.95)

JEAN AYRES NOTECARD SET

Jean Ayres was a talented artist. With her family's permission we have reproduced four of her watercolors into sets of eight notecards and envelopes. All of the net profits from sales of these notecard sets are donated to furthering research of dysfunction in sensory integration. $9.95/set.

A. JEAN AYRES BOOKS AVAILABLE FROM:

Western Psychological Services
12031 Wilshire Blvd.
Los Angeles, CA 90025-1251
800-648-8857 (U.S. and Canada)
310-478-2061
www.wpspublish.com

Sensory Integration and the Child

by A. Jean Ayres, PhD

This helpful book translates the author's pioneering research on sensory integration into language that parents and teachers can easily understand. With uncommon sensitivity to the needs and concerns of those who care for developmentally delayed children, Dr. Ayres explains sensory integrative dysfunction, then tells the reader how to recognize it and what to do about it. Also included are a glossary of terms related to sensory integration and an extremely useful question-and-answer section. Indispensable reading for parents, this book is also an excellent way to improve communication between therapist, parents, and teachers. Paperbound, 191 pp. $24.50.

Sensory Integration and Learning Disorders by A. Jean Ayres, Ph.D.

This book presents a model of sensory integrative processes and their malfunctions in children as well as a specific intervention program stressing control of sensory input and the development of adaptive responses through purposeful activities. The volume offers useful information for all professionals concerned with children who have sensory integrative dysfunction, including special educators, psychologists, and occupational therapists. 294 pp. $69.50.

Another Critically-acclaimed Title from Crestport Press

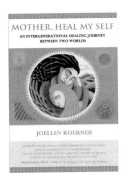

Mother, Heal My Self:
An Intergenerational Journey
Between Two Worlds
By JoEllen Koerner, PhD, RN, FAAN

"This extraordinary book reminds us, that when it comes to the healing of the body and soul, we are all indigenous people. This is a true story, told from the heart like a prayer that reveals how we too can become the heroes of our own healing journey."

Carl A. Hammerschlag, M.D.
Author: *The Dancing Healers*

JoEllen Koerner was raised in a small Mennonite community in South Dakota, became a Civil Rights activist in the South, and rose to prominence as a nurse executive of international repute. None of these life experiences, or her honed skills as a Western medical practitioner, prepared her for the moment every parent hopes never happens: Her daughter, Kristi, her body wracked with pain, asks permission to die. Into the depths of this dreaded moment enters Wanigi Waci (Spirit Dancer), a dear friend and keeper of the Lakota Sioux healing traditions. He invites Kristi and JoEllen into his People's time-honored healing ways and giving community, with ramifications whose importance ultimately surpasses the restoration of Kristi's health.

This wonderful book has helped many find the strength to face their own health challenges. 212 pages; $14.95.